DAVID

TO Sheldon

STAY True to
Your Purpose!

ONE DEGREE

UNLEASHING YOUR **FOCUS**

GARY L. WILDER

WESTBOW
PRESS®
A DIVISION OF THOMAS NELSON
& ZONDERVAN

WestBow Press books may be ordered through booksellers or by contacting:

WestBow Press
A Division of Thomas Nelson & Zondervan
1663 Liberty Drive
Bloomington, IN 47403
www.westbowpress.com
844-714-3454

ISBN: 978-1-6642-1360-9 (sc)
ISBN: 978-1-6642-1361-6 (hc)
ISBN: 978-1-6642-1359-3 (e)

Library of Congress Control Number: 2020923381

Printed in the United States of America.

WestBow Press rev. date: 02/12/2021

Contents

Foreword

In Genesis 11:6 (KJV), the Lord says, "Nothing will be restrained from them, which they have imagined to do." *One Degree* takes you through the process by which your dreams, desires, and imaginations may become a reality.

Gary Wilder is not a man of words, but one of action. As you will discover, his approach to life is one of striving to win in all things. This is made evident in *One Degree*, as he shares the truths of his life as a dreamer, Marine, husband, father, and minister.

He has written a practical step-by-step approach on how to be all that God created you to be. For every individual starting on their life's journey—or wanting to get back on course—this is a must-read book.

Bishop R. W. Thomas, DD

Preface

"Alpha One, this is Charlie 3. The objective is a house located at grid 19368437. How copy, over?"

"I copy. The objective is a house located at grid 19368437."

Before receiving the objective, my Heavy Machine Gun Platoon and I were instructed to provide protection for the convoy that was following. We were informed not to engage unless we were detected and fired upon. The above scenario was a training mission to prepare for the real event.

Although this book is not about the operational mission, if our platoon did not know where we were going and, more importantly, we did not follow the coordinates correctly, we would have gotten off the path and ended up in the wrong location. This could have been dangerous for us and our fellow Marines.

Just being one degree off for each hundred meters traveled could lead to a disastrous mission.

Knowing where we are going is important for all of us. Oftentimes we get off track by veering in the wrong direction. However, we can get back on course by navigating to the correct location. During field week of Marine Corps boot camp, every recruit must go through land navigation training. Regardless of Military Occupational Specialty (MOS), every Marine is considered a basic rifleman or infantry Marine. Marine Corps insignias emphasize this fact. Every enlisted rank insignia, with the exception of Private or Private First Class (PFC), First Sergeant, Master Gunnery Sergeant, and Sergeant Major, bears crossed rifles as a sign that they are a rifleman. As a basic rifleman, every Marine must understand navigation, that is, how to get from one point to another correctly.

Throughout my nearly twenty-three years in the United States Marine Corps, focusing on where I wanted to go was not an option. As a Marine, and my focus had to be on where the Corps was directing me. Whether I was on an operation, conducting day-to-day training, or pursuing promotions, maintaining focus was the key to fulfilling that mission.

During my time in the Corps, I served in a variety of MOSs from Radio Operator, Combat Arms (Machine Gunner), Infantry Leader, Scout Sniper, Drill Instructor, and Counterintelligence. Each of these jobs required a different focus. I maintained a level of success in each of these positions and received promotions as a result of keeping my focus. I want to encourage you that regardless of what you are doing in life, you can obtain success by sustaining your focus.

We all have our one-degree moments. A turning point takes us either in the right or, unfortunately, wrong direction. I have talked to successful people all over the United States and abroad and found that each of them has had a one-degree moment. They were headed down the wrong highway, but someone intervened and helped them correct their course. Consider the following:

- One young man was on the verge of prison, but a judge saw something in him and showed him mercy. He got back on the right path and became a successful military man.
- A young lady was on the verge of homelessness, but someone gave her a job, and she became a skilled manager.
- A grandmother found her grandson selling drugs, and she spoke into his life. His course correction led to him becoming a successful preacher.

We all can have that moment of decision, but it is up to each of us to choose to correct our path so we can fulfill what we are created to do.

I desire that this book will help you to focus on the future. It does not matter if you are an entrepreneur, business manager, receptionist, nurse, warehouse worker, computer programmer, waitress, or actor. Each of us needs to focus on our destiny.

This is not a how-to book about focus, but simply a guide to help you stay on the path that will lead to you fulfilling your purpose and destiny through focus.

Remember, one degree over a period of years can lead you away from where you desire to go. May something in this book stir your dreams, imagination, and desire to go to the next level in your life.

Acknowledgments

First and foremost, I want to thank my wife and friend, Minister Felecia Wilder. I cannot overstate the impact she has had over my life with her love, prayers, support, and wisdom with this project and many others. Her devotion to her Lord, family, and church are a shining example of a life lived well.

I want to acknowledge others in my life who mentored me into the man I am today: my parents, Ellen (Wilder) McCormick and the late Joe T. Wilder and maternal and paternal grandparents, Robert and Willie Mae Beasley and Allen and Pearl Wilder. Additionally, I want to include my stepdad, deacon and former Army First Sergeant John McCormick for his continued support of this project.

Likewise, I want to acknowledge my children, Stephén, Gary II, and Alexis. You all are the reason I do what I do. My dream is to leave a legacy for you all to follow and for you to duplicate this for future generations.

Direction 1
The Few, the Proud

Let the Focus Begin

The time had arrived. The Marine Gunnery Sergeant (Gunny) called me and said it was time to ship off to boot camp. They sent me, along with other recruits, to the Military Entrance Processing Station (MEPS) in Charlotte, North Carolina. Anticipation filled us as to what lay ahead of us at Parris Island, South Carolina.

We were taken to the airport, where we boarded a plane to South Carolina. We arrived at the airport around 4:30 p.m. and remained there for several hours, waiting for other recruits to arrive from across the country. It was a warm, late-summer night, but it promised a slight chill. About 9:30 p.m., a bus arrived, and a tall figure, dressed in a sharply creased khaki and green uniform, approached us and told us to stand near the bus.

Fifty young men and I entered the bus. The hour was late, and most of us had been awake since 5:30 a.m. We were wondering when we would get a chance to get some rest. The answer seemed to be, "Not anytime soon."

In North Carolina, the skies would turn an eerie greenish-yellow color as a forewarning of a storm, and it would seem that everything around you would get quiet and relatively calm. You knew that something was brewing over the horizon but weren't quite sure what it was or when it was going to hit. This was the feeling I had as we boarded the bus. It was calm, but I knew something was coming. I just did not know when it would hit or where.

As we took our bus ride to our final destination, we began to smell something that would never leave our senses, the odor of the swamp. It is a unique smell, one that reinforced that the storm was getting closer. I began to wonder, *Where are they taking us? What kind of place are we going to?*

The bus stopped, and we thought we had arrived at our destination, but the journey was just beginning. We tried to get some sleep, but anticipation didn't allow it. After riding for what felt like another hour or so through dark, winding roads and our nostrils filling with that unique sulfur smell, the bus stopped again. This time it did not move.

The door opened, and another figure appeared. The storm had arrived.

Reality set in, and I knew that I had arrived at Marine Corps Recruit Depot, Parris Island, South Carolina, and I had just been introduced to one of the meanest individuals on the planet, a Marine Drill Instructor! He came on the bus like a Tasmanian devil! All I remember him saying was, "Get your bodies off this bus and stand on the yellow footprints!"

The storm intensified as we got off the bus. Several other Tasmanian devils were waiting for us. I thought to myself, *This is not home anymore!*

Marine boot camp is a life-changing transformation for all who dare to enter through its gates. It is a fast-paced, dizzying, double-time regimen that takes you from youth to young adult in a ninety-five-day process. It culminates with an event called the crucible, which stretches, fortifies, and enhances your mind, body, and spirit. Experiencing the crucible brings about teamwork, camaraderie, and the ability to place trust in your fellow Marine. That is what makes us a band of brothers.

Just the mention of the term "boot camp" brings fear to some and a sense of challenge to others. When people think about a Marine, they often think of a highly motivated, truly dedicated, physically fit, and sometimes high-strung individual, which is all true to some extent. Marines have to have an attitude of never saying defeat, regardless of the circumstance, and considering ourselves "lean, mean, green, fighting machines." To complete the rigors of Marine Corps boot camp, you must have a keen focus to endure the day-to-day stress. As we often say, it is 90 percent mental and 10 percent physical.

Boot camp has four phases. The first three weeks are designed to cleanse you of all traces of civilian life and completely indoctrinate you into the ways of the Marine Corps. The first two phases prepare you for the third phase, where every Marine must learn how to survive in the field and study land navigation, that is, how to get from one point to another. Land navigation requires that you know how to calculate a grid azimuth, intersection, resection, and back azimuth.

Now what is an azimuth? I thought when I first heard it. I was sure I would get lost trying to get from one point to another using a compass and trying to calculate these formulas.

In a robotic voice, the instructor explained, "An azimuth is the direction of a celestial object from the observer, expressed as the angular distance from the north or south point of the horizon to the point at which a vertical circle passing through the object intersects the horizon."

All of the other recruits and I seemed to have the same thought, *Unless he breaks this down, we are going to end up in another state.* He must have heard our thoughts and simply said, "It is the direction between me and a fixed object." That seemed to make more sense than the celestial point.

Over a few days, we learned that the object is to get within thirty feet of your objective. Getting within three feet is even better.

Basically, knowing the direction you are going is essential to hitting your mark.

When I was in Desert Shield/Desert Storm (the Gulf War), it was challenging to point to an object when I was standing in the middle of the desert and all I could see in a 360-degree circle was desert. Although we were introduced to electronic navigation during Desert Storm, at times I had to rely on the map and compass to get from one point to another when there was not a permanent fixture (like a building) on which to point the compass. I would find the fixture on the map and set the grid azimuth to point us in the right direction.

In today's military, most of the navigation is performed electronically; however, in the event the electronic device has an error, knowing how to use the basic map and compass is vital to get from one point to another.

Ordinarily when patrolling to my destination, I must try to stay true to my mark. Drifting one degree off the mark can be harmful. One degree doesn't seem like it will make a big difference. But over a long distance, being off by just one degree means there is a chance of missing my objective. For instance, when traveling 3,280 feet (just over a half-mile), being off one degree means that you could find yourself fifty-six feet (or nineteen yards) to the left or right of your intended target. Again, that may not seem like a lot, but track that over, say, ten miles, and it will put you off target by 0.17 miles (or 898 feet). That can mean life or death for a unit you are supporting.

Courage points us in the right direction. For any leader, strength requires focused energy just as being courageous requires mental toughness. Ideally having strength and courage takes lots of willpower and focus. In Oren Harari's book *The Leadership Secrets of*

Colin Powell, Powell is very specific that leadership requires "moral, physical, mental, and spiritual courage."[1]

As a Marine, I had no choice but to have moral and physical courage, encompassed with mental and physical strength, along with a keen sense of focus. It kept me thriving during nearly twenty-three years of service. Focus, strength, and power were synonymous with my lifestyle. Lacking any of these elements was not a choice; I had to have them all.

Comparably, the mindset of the Marine Corps is to attack. Our fighting spirit is a trait that says, "Charge ahead!" Our (Marine Corps) history defines us—

> What sets Marines apart from any other fighting force on the globe isn't just how they're trained, the equipment they use or their tactics. It's something much more primal—it's the fighting spirit that lives within every Marine and drives them to accept nothing less than victory in all situations. That determination to win, eagerness to fight, and a high standard of excellence are all traits strengthened in the Corps.[2]

This fighting spirit and focus are instilled in every Marine during recruit training at either Recruit Depot Parris Island, South Carolina; Recruit Depot San Diego, California; or Officer Candidates School in Quantico, Virginia. It is an experience that lasts a lifetime.

One Degree

When I set my sights on a target, I have to maintain motivation along with focus to reach my destination.

My motivation may be there, but the question is: Do I listen to the advice of others or do my own thing? Losing motivation and focus can cause me to lose hope in what I believe I want to accomplish. It seems like days keep piling onto days, to the point where I lose sight of where I am going. When days turn into months and months into years, there seems to be no hope or direction. I start to feel off course, which could lead me to feeling that there is no purpose.

Remember that traveling just one degree off my intended destination over a distance could land me away from my mark. In order to understand how to hit the mark, I had to get instructions. I had to be willing to be taught how to navigate with precision. This, of course, means allowing a mentor to give me guidance on how to get to my destination without hitting any pitfalls. I have to pay close attention to my mentor's every word, or I will find myself off the mark.

When I was in high school, I listened to all kinds of voices. Many of the voices were telling me to do things that were not right in God's eyes, activities that were not doing anything useful for my purpose. I grew up as an only child, and oftentimes I was searching for a big brother to guide or direct me. Unfortunately, at times I listened to the wrong voices, those that led to a path of destruction rather than success. I began listening to the wrong voices and doing all the wrong things that led me many degrees off my intended mark.

The Power of a Question

In my junior year of high school, I was on the high school football team and had just finished our annual inter-team red-and-white scrimmage game. After the game, I was hanging out with my teammates having a great time, doing things I should not have been involved in. It was getting late, and one of my teammates gave me a ride home. I did not know it, but he had been drinking excessively.

He started speeding, and I said, "Hey, slow down!"

He laughed and sped up. We were heading toward a sharp curve when I yelled, "We are about ..."

My next memory is him lying unconscious in my lap and someone screaming, "Are they all right?" I could not move. Later I was told that the car had rolled over several times and hit a pole. Fortunately we both survived the crash, but barely. It is only through God's mercy that I am here to tell my story.

Fast-forward a couple months. I'd had two surgeries and was home recovering when a good friend of the family, the late Evangelist Joshua Caleb Hoskins, came to our house at 202 Brown Street. He and I talked for a while, and then he began to point out things leading me away from the purpose God had for my life. He made it clear that I could have died that night.

He said, "God has other plans for you instead."

He did not use any type of scare tactics but simply shared his story and talked about life with me that day. As we talked, he asked me an important question, one that would transform my life forever.

He asked, "Do you want to receive Jesus into your life today? Again, you could have been killed in that crash, but He has given you another chance to get right with Him. Do you want to accept Him in your life today?"

Up to that point, I went to church and could talk about Christ, but I did not have a personal relationship with Him. Despite my fear and without reservation, I answered Evangelist Hoskins, "Yes!" I accepted Christ that day, September 20, 1978. Evangelist Hoskins became a mentor for my life until God called him home in 2008.

The person speaking into your life is like a tribal leader. They give insight that will help the entire tribe and not the individual alone. Dave Logan states, "As a Tribal Leader you need to speak the language as an insider. Only then can you build trust with a tribe at this stage and use leverage points to advance it."[3]

This was the case with Evangelist Hoskins. Because of his direction and mentorship, I was able to see when I was headed down the wrong path and moving away from my destination of success. Although I accepted Christ, oftentimes I missed the mark. The temptations in this world were strong, and I strayed away at times. However, because Evangelist Hoskins had given me a moral compass, I knew how to shoot a resection and get back on track.

This is what the instructor for land navigation was doing for us during boot camp, showing us how to stay on course. It is the same for a mentor who speaks into our life. Bill Hull shared, "Throughout history, mentors or spiritual guides have helped temper people's tendency to be lazy, lose focus, or give into temptation."[4]

The person speaking into my life must build a rapport so the spoken words can resonate inside of me. That person, directly and indirectly, can become a mentor to me, which will bring success to my life. Evangelist Hoskins became such an individual for me.

How the Journey Started

When things got a little rough, my dad would often say, "There would be days like this!"

Growing up in Thomasville, North Carolina, in a little yellow, two-bedroom, wood-frame house, I remember my dad, the late Joe (J. T.) Wilder, talk about displaying strength as he shared about growing up in the segregated South during the 1940s and 1950s. He was a slender, muscular man, about six feet tall, with a smooth, tenor voice. He told us about working in the cotton field with my granddad and baling nearly two hundred pounds of cotton.

One summer when I was in middle school, my family and I were traveling through his home state of South Carolina. My mom was driving, and we were passing a cotton field. Dad urgently spoke to her, "Pull over and stop!" We thought something was wrong. He told me to get out and go to the cotton field and pick a cotton boll.

We did as he told us, and then he said somberly, "I want you to know that is the closest that you will ever get to picking cotton!"

Dad went on to tell of the hard times he and his brothers endured in those types of fields with Papa (my granddad, Allen Wilder). Although my dad never served in the military, he had to have the physical and mental courage to endure a lot growing up during those times, which helped to develop his leadership.

As I reflected on the leadership my dad exuded, I realized I did not see it as a youth or young adult, but the older I got, the more I see it. And I often experience it when I mentor my sons, male youth, and young adult men. Watching his work ethic and leadership inspired me to want to do more and be an inspiration to others.

When my dad and I were together, working in the yard or just sitting around talking, he often spoke about family and friends who served in the military. He had tried to enlist, but due to an injury he suffered as a teen, it prevented him from joining. While playing with friends, he fell from a tree and broke his collarbone, preventing him from lifting his left arm above his head. (It didn't prevent him from whipping my behind when I did something wrong, but that's another story!) I knew he always regretted not being able to serve.

Likewise, Papa, just as my dad did, would often talk about family members who served in the military. Everyone who served would send Papa their boot camp or basic training photos. He kept them in a large frame that hung in his bedroom on Bowerwood Drive.

That was one of my second homes, with him and my grandmother (Mama), Pearl.

Papa was the leader of the family. Everyone respected his leadership and would come to him for any issue. He was the glue that kept the family intact and in order. He was not a tall man, about five-foot-six or five-foot-seven, but was very strong with a very athletic build. Even as he aged and developed a slight bend at the waist, his voice was forceful and a little shaky due to a mild case of Parkinson's disease.

When I was at Papa's house, he would call me into the bedroom, point to a picture, and tell me the story of each person, where they served or were serving at that time. He, like my dad, did not serve in the military but had a great admiration for those who did. I never got tired of hearing the stories, even if he would change it up or sometimes exaggerate a little.

Listening to him allowed me to think about what it would be like to serve. He had an extra love for those in the Marine Corps. I wondered if he were pushing me in that direction. If so, it was the best path he could have pushed me.

Papa began telling me these adventures when I was in the fifth grade. A year later, I wrote to the Marine Corps about joining. Of course, their answer was to graduate high school and then write again. During my junior year, I lost interest in the military. When you read the next chapter, you will see what happened.

Dad could lead our family and extended family. He was not a perfect man, but who is? He was not a completely spiritual man, but he did know that Jesus was the head of his life. When things were at their toughest, he knew who to call on for guidance and strength. I would hear him mention his favorite scripture when he needed that strength, Psalm 23:1–2 (KJV), "The Lord is my shepherd ... He leads me ..."

One event is etched in my memory. When Papa passed away in 1979, after lowering my grandfather into the ground, my dad stood in front of his brothers and sisters at the gravesite and said, "I am the leader of this family now." He demonstrated it to the family until God called him home in 1988.

His leadership stirred me to want to be a part of the Marine Corps to develop that leadership and work ethic in myself. I joined the Corps in June 1980, and my dad was very proud when I marched across the field on August 29, 1980, as a Marine. Joining the Corps gave my dad the chance to live through me something he was not able to experience. To see the joy in his eyes when I graduated is something I will never forget.

Who Speaks into Your Life?

As I mentioned earlier about Papa, my next home was with my maternal granddad, Robert Beasley (Granddaddy) and grandmother (Grandma) Willie Mae Beasley. His words of wisdom were instrumental to me. As I look back, Granddaddy was a mentor to me as well. I learned so much about patience sitting with him and Grandma in the backyard on Tremont Street in Thomasville.

Granddaddy was a tall man, about six-foot-two or six-foot-three, with a slim, athletic build. I used to ask if he played basketball, but he was an avid baseball player. Although he never served in the military, he would not only share about those who served, like his son, but he also spoke on God's favor and blessings to me.

When I think about favor, I remember once when Granddaddy found favor. He had retired from the furniture industry and began a lawn and landscaping business. I would often work with him. One of his jobs was with a wealthy family in Thomasville. While working for them, the man of the family was impressed with Granddaddy's work on his yard. He would often give extra money to Granddaddy and offer gifts to our family as well.

During this time, Granddaddy was having trouble with his car, a light-blue Chevrolet Biscayne, which he had to constantly work on. One afternoon, the man of the family asked Granddaddy if he would pick up a car for him from the Pontiac/Buick dealership. Granddaddy agreed and drove it back to their house.

When we returned, he asked Granddaddy, "How did it drive?"

"Really nice and smooth."

"That's great! The new car is yours!"

Granddaddy was a proud man and did not like being given anything, but this time he had no choice. The man insisted, and Granddaddy had a new car, a black Buick Skylark. That's favor!

> *"A good name is to be chosen rather than great riches, and favor is better than silver and gold"* Proverbs 22:1 (ESV).

Granddaddy was a mentor to me. When a mentor finds favor, that favor can transfer to the mentee at some point in their life. Granddaddy is now at the feet of Christ. From me sitting at Granddaddy's feet, I have found favor in my life throughout the years.

To stay true to my destination, I needed assistance from mentors who could speak into my life. Let me emphasize that a mentor is someone who guides you, not someone there to be a friend. They are there to assist with character development. Martin Sanders wrote, "Ministry in general and mentoring in particular, can be summarized in this same way. As emerging leaders are mentored through stages of personal, spiritual and emotional development, character formation takes center stage."[5]

Having that person in my life to assist in navigating through some of life's pitfalls is very important. I am thankful for those individuals who planted a nugget that kept me on the right course.

At times I had to find a mentor; other times a mentor was right in front of me. But it wasn't until years later that I realized they were mentors for me. For example, my father would consistently deposit words of wisdom into my life, but it wasn't until years after he passed that I began to use those words to assist in situations I had to overcome.

The older I get, the wiser my father is becoming.

Mentoring is developing relationships and guiding us to become better in our lives. The original mentor was a character in Homer and Butler, *The Odyssey*, in which the "Greek soldier, Odysseus, is called to war against Troy. Odysseus leaves his young son, Telemachus, in the hands of his friend/slave, Mentor. Mentor was left in charge of everything with full authority over the servants."[6]

Just as Mentor was there for Telemachus, mentors today should be an experienced and trusted advisor for those they counsel. Having a trusted person speak into my life was key to shaping my development.

I want to share with you the people who assisted with my development. As you read this list, take a moment to replace the names I mention with people in your life. If you see a gap or you did not have people who helped you, use this list as a catalyst for searching for those trusted, wise people for yourself.

In my early years, several people made an impact on me. I did not realize it at the time that their wisdom was a mentoring session.

For instance, both sets of my grandparents, Robert and Willie Mae Beasley and Allen and Pearl Wilder, showed me how to rely on God and work hard. My father displayed how to provide and be committed to the family by leading.

My mom, Ellen (Wilder) McCormick, displayed creativity, a voice of reason, and knowledge of how to care for the family. To this day, she continues to be a voice of reason in my life. She ensures that family is always first and passes that same nurturing down to her grandchildren, along with teaching them the creative side of life. Plus, the woman can stretch a meal from Sunday to Sunday and make it taste just as fresh as the day it was cooked.

I have to share this. I know she will get me later. When I was younger, my dad bought several whole chickens. One week, my mom cooked chicken in every conceivable way it could be.

On the fourth day of having a chicken dish, my dad looked at her and said, "Woman, if we have chicken one more time, we are going to start growing wings!"

Needless to say, that was the last chicken meal for a while. That is the creative side of my mother, and she has passed it along to my children and me. (Well, not cooking chicken every day.)

I received counsel from uncles and aunts who guided me with military knowledge, information on having a successful marriage, and guidance through political and entrepreneurial spirit. Other family members have assisted in helping my focus and growth. Martin Sanders continued, "Resource people can come from various places. They can be relatives and family members."[7]

> *Don't devalue wisdom from people because of familiarity.*

The mentoring did not stop during my adult and Marine Corps years. Those who gave me a word to help me focus on my future were Marines I served with, specifically Sergeant Major Lorin Rhaney (more on his story later).

There were church leaders I served with over the years, including my current spiritual leader and mentor, Bishop Rick Thomas, DD, who pushed me to complete this project and many others to come. These individuals are memorable because they dropped wisdom into my life that keeps me focused on the right direction. They are and were like coaches in my life.

Matthew Floding from Duke Divinity School instructs, "Great coaches give their teams direction and motivation to help them to reach their goals."[8] Permitting the right people to speak into my life allowed my dreams to come and to stay alive.

Direction 2
D-R-E-A-M-S

While eating dinner at the family table our son, Gary II, said to my wife and I that he dreamed he would live in Japan. At the time he was a thirteen-year-old middle-schooler when we lived in Fredericksburg, Virginia, and stationed at Quantico Marine Base.

We were not sure how to take what he said, but we encouraged him to reach for that dream. More than seven years later, now living in Margate, Florida, his dream manifested when he joined the Marine Corps, and after boot camp and his MOS school, he was given orders to Okinawa, Japan. He served the next four years in that country. His dream of living in Japan came alive, and he fulfilled that dream and much more.

Dreams can be the essence of who we are. Pastor Joel Osteen says, "God's way is better than your way. His plan is bigger than your plan. His dream for your life is more rewarding, more fulfilling, better than you've ever dreamed of. Now stay open and let God do it His way."[9]

When we dream, we take ourselves out of the realm of reality and into a world where we can become greater. We nurtured our son's dream, and it took him further than he imagined. When we dream, we look at what could be rather than what is.

It is very disheartening when someone comes along and tries to discourage our dreams. Usually they are non-dreamers, and because they do not have a dream, they come along to steal others' dreams. They have no vision for their own lives—perhaps someone stole their dreams—and now they want to do the same to others. They ask, "Why should we reach for something? Let me settle for the status quo." Disappointed with their own lives, these non-visionaries/dreamers must not be allowed to impact our dreams.

Our dreams may seem slow in coming into manifestation; however, if we continue to believe in them, they will surely come to pass. Proverbs 13:12 (NLT) says, "Hope deferred makes the heart sick, but a dream fulfilled is a tree of life."

Dreams can be deferred or delayed, and it may seem like they will never come to pass; nevertheless, if we stay focused on what God placed inside of us, that dream will blossom. The dream that God gives us should become the driving force of our life. He has a purpose for each of us, and the dream is the catalyst to discovering that purpose, just as it was for my son.

Some may have a dream, but what they dream may not be in their DNA to accomplish. Consider the anonymous story of the little turtle who dreamed of flying. Every day the little turtle would climb a tree, and once he reached the top, he would jump off, throw out his little legs, flap with all his might, and then, of course, hit the ground with a loud thud. After resting in that position for a few minutes, he would repeat the process with the same results.

Watching in the distance were birds, a male and female robin. The male said to the female, "I don't care what you say. I'm going to tell him he's a turtle."

The turtle had a misguided concept of his dream. No matter how much he tried, his dream of flying was not in his DNA. We must ensure that our dreams are realistic. For instance, if you dream of being a medical surgeon and you have a fear of seeing someone operated on, that may not be the dream that God has for you unless He relieves you of that fear.

Allow Him to instill the dream that will fulfill your purpose and destiny.

Block Out the Noise

When I was in the sixth grade, I dreamed of being a Marine. I was determined to become one. I sent off a mailer card requesting information, and they wrote back and said, "Graduate from high school."

I wrote again in the eighth grade and received the same reply. My sophomore year, I got the same results. Late in my junior year and into my senior year, some of my peers began to ask, "Why do you want to go to the military? Go to college or get a job."

Their influence began to turn me away from my dream, and I started to seek out colleges. The Marines called and wrote to me, but I stopped pursuing my dream because of what others were feeding me. But my dream was just dormant. It wasn't dead!

Two months before my high school graduation, the fire inside of me rekindled. One afternoon I drove to the Marine Recruiting Office, in High Point, North Carolina, and met with the Gunnery Sergeant.

Without any hesitation, I said to him, "I want to be in boot camp no more than two weeks after I graduate. If that can't happen, I will not join the Marine Corps."

He walked to his board, called his unit headquarters, and then took another recruit's name off the board and placed mine on top. While I was in his office, he called the other recruit and informed him, "Your ship date has changed."

I graduated from high school on June 5 and shipped to Parris Island on June 10.

> *When a dream is inside of you, block out the noise,*
> *and allow God to stir up your dream.*

My God-given dreams determined my destiny. God's dream for my life shaped me into the kind of person that He wanted me to become. There are no great people, only ordinary people committed to great dreams. Committing to a great dream draws something out of you that allows you to become larger than you would have without the dream.

God uses dreams in our lives to direct, shape, and define us. That is what He did for me by stirring up that dormant dream. Martin Sanders challenges us with this statement and questions,

> As you look at future dreams, ask yourself the following questions. All of these come together to create a life plan for you. The goal is to invest the life you have been given in such a way that it creates the greatest impact on the kingdom of God and in eternity:

- What else is there for me?
- Is there one more big challenge? Is there a mission or task that I need to undertake that I have not yet done?
- Is there something that no one else is doing that I can do?
- What maturity and development do I need in order to be able to do it?
- Do I have a unique perspective, calling or purpose in life that could be used in ways I have not thought of? In ways that perhaps others have not thought of, either?
- What will be the lasting impact of my life? How can I begin to plan for it now?
- What resources do I need in order to fulfill my mission(s)? People resources? Financial resources? Educational resources? Experiential resources?[10]

Our dreams determine our dignity. How do you feel about yourself? If you don't have a dream for your life right now, you may feel like you're just existing. Unfortunately I encounter people all the time who ask, "Why am I here? What am I here for? Why do I get up in the morning? Why do I go to work? What's the purpose of life?"

No dream means no esteem.

Once God's dream manifests itself inside of you, then the plan He has for you comes alive. Christ can be the nucleus of your dream. Having God as the center of your dream will stir up the gifts He has planted within you.

When dreams are not manifested inside of us, we become sick and eventually sad. Again, Proverbs 13:12 (NKJV) instructs us, "Hope or a dream deferred makes the heart sick: but when the desire comes, it is a tree of life."

This scripture reminds me of the poem by Langston Hughes, "A Dream Deferred." One line of the poem asks, "Does it (a dream) dry up like a raisin in the sun?"[11]

When a person has a dream burning inside of them, they will sometimes neglect food itself! I am not saying to deny yourself food or nourishments, but when your dream turns into passion, you may go without until it is accomplished. Husbands and wives, come together and dream together. Don't have a heated discussion with your spouse when they have a dream but come into agreement together and nourish the dream. Families begin to dream again.

The Acronym

In the military world, we live by acronyms. An acronym takes a word and breaks it down into letters to make a word. For instance, let's use the word *dream* to show how God can manifest that dream inside of you:

D: Dedicate Your Life to God

When I dedicate something, I devote it to the worship of a divine being or set it apart for sacred use. My dream should be set apart for sacred use. I have to be willing to dedicate my life to God so He can show me where that dream is located within me.

Do not allow others to squeeze you into their mold; let God transform you. Most of us miss God's dream because we are not looking at Him. We're looking at someone else's dream. We want to be like our neighbors, our friends, or some famous person.

> *But God wrote our dream before the foundation of the world was laid. It is uniquely designed for us.*

"Let us run with perseverance the race marked out for us" (Hebrews 12:1 NIV). God has a particular course for you to run. No one else can run it but you. If you are always looking at other people's dreams, you are going to end up running their race and not your own.

R: Reserve Time to Nurture Your Dream

I have to spend time alone with God in order to hear Him speak to me about my dreams. At times I was busy on social media, inundated with negative news, politics, and the like, and I was not spending time in pursuit of my dreams.

Balswick and Balswick stated, "Those who are most satisfied engage in rewarding activities and reserve time for themselves."[12] If I want to hear what God is saying to me about my dreams and see what He is showing me about my vision, I must turn off things that are distracting me. To hear from God, I had to set an appointed time and place with Him and spend quality time with my heavenly Father. Spending time with family is important; however, I must find that quiet time with God to secure my dream. This allows me to reflect on the dream and vision He is painting on my mind.

E: Evaluate Yourself and Your Abilities

We have to ensure that our dreams are in line with our abilities. Growing up in North Carolina, one of my dreams was to become a race car driver. This dream began when I had the opportunity in elementary school to meet a local racing legend at an event. He allowed me to sit in his car and showed me some of the vehicle's features. That did it! I wanted to be a race car driver!

I went to a few racing events but never had the exposure to learn the sport. I understood myself and my abilities enough to know that this was not the direction that life was leading me. I am still an avid race car fan, but the dream of being a professional is behind me.

I want to just take a brief moment on the word *exposure*. To get the dream activated, we must have exposure to the thing that can fuel the dream. Possibly if I had exposure to the racing world, it could have become a reality.

> *If you have a dream and it is your passion, find a way to get exposed to that dream to assist in making it a reality.*

I, along with a team of men, mentor young males between the ages of thirteen through eighteen through a group mentoring organization, Men2Boys, in Margate, Florida. One of our core subjects deals with dreams. During my mentoring sessions with the teens, I inquire, "What are your dreams?" The number-one answer is, "I want to be a professional football player." Getting the football answer is standard since football is king in Florida.

Our next question is, "Are you currently on a football team or getting training, and if not, what are you doing to make this dream a reality?"

The majority of the teens are not on a team or doing anything that will make their dream become a reality. They are not getting the right exposure to make this dream come alive, or it is not in their DNA, like the turtle, to accomplish that part of their dream.

We do not squash their dreams; however, we bring them to the realization that if they are not doing anything to work toward their dream, it will quickly become a nightmare.

That is the case with some adults. Many have dreamed of being a business owner but have never taken a business class or learned what it takes to run a business. Most have not even worked in the type of business that they would like to own. If I am not doing anything that is bringing my dreams into the realm of reality, then I need to wake up.

One of our leadership principles in the Marine Corps is "Know yourself and seek self-improvement."[13] Whatever I dream about, I first have to confirm that it is aligned with the gift that God has placed within me.

2 Corinthians 13:5 (NASB) tells us that we are to "test yourselves to see if you are in the faith; examine yourselves!" Examining ourselves allows us to improve on any deficiencies we may have.

> *Understand that you are a work of art. You are unique. There is nobody like you. You didn't come off an assembly line. You were not created to be second class. You were created to be special. You are God's leading lady or man, and you are unique.*

However, there's more to life than just being unique. God wants you to be uniquely effective in what He has designed you for. He designed you to do the good deeds for which He fashioned you. Even before you were born, God proposed a role for your life. He gave you certain gifts, abilities, and talents to serve Him and others. Know that your abilities are in line with the dream that God has for your life.

A: Associate with People Who Have Dreams

I often hear stories of people who are excited about a new venture or a particular job that sought it and got it. Some have dreamed of doing something that is out of the ordinary or even extraordinary. They may have wanted to be an actor, lawyer, doctor, or the like, and when they run into an obstacle along the way, they sometimes tell their problems to non-dreamers.

The non-dreamer tells them, "This is not for you; do something else instead."

The end results could be devastating when the person gives up on their dream and does not pursue their passion. This almost happened to me. Someone nearly talked me out of my dream and passion. Does this sound familiar? Someone crushes a dream before it has a chance to catch root.

If I am going to dream, it is essential that I hang out with people who are also trying to discover God's dream for their lives.

Both dreams and discouragement are contagious.

The people who are closest to me will either help develop God's dream for my life or hinder my dream. There is no such thing as a neutral person. I am in charge of choosing the people who are closest to me. I have known individuals who missed their dream because a family member or friend had no interest in it.

Let me explain. A man told me that he was seeking new opportunities. He found one and was offered his dream job in another state. I encouraged him to make the move, and he stated that he would be moving in a couple months.

We had not talked for a few months, so I called to check on his progress. About three months passed, and he was still in the area.

I inquired, "Why haven't you made the move?"

After some hemming and hawing, he stated, "I've been talking with some family members, and they convinced me that making a move wouldn't be good. They said I could do the same by staying at home."

However, that didn't work out for him. We kept in touch periodically throughout the year. He was still in his hometown and extremely miserable. The hometown job had cut back on work. The opportunity for the dream job never came again. He listened to the wrong counsel, people who were non-dreamers.

If I want God's dream for my life, I have to be around godly dreamers. A godly dreamer will encourage me to be and have everything that God has designed for me. They will help me reach my God-given potential.

Proverbs 27:17 (NLT) states, "As iron sharpens iron, so a friend sharpens a friend." If I want to soar with the eagles, I can't run with turkeys. If I want to break out of a rut, I have to change my friends and associates. If they are not helping me to grow, then they need to go!

M: Make Your Dream Public

My wife, Felecia, and I often share ideas and dreams with each other. I know that she will nurture my dreams and I will nurture hers. We believe in one another. Tell your dream to someone who will hold you accountable for your dream.

> *In other words, don't tell your dream to a non-dreamer. They will only kill and destroy that dream.*

Share your dream with those who will help catapult it to another level.

Dr. King shared his dream with the world and made it public. It catapulted him into the annals of time and halls of history. His dream resonated with those who heard it then, and it still reverberates today. Many have nurtured his dream and allowed God to be in the midst of bringing it to manifestation.

By telling dreamers about my dream, I'm making a statement of faith that will allow them to come alongside me and become a part of it.

> First, I see it, then I sense it, and lastly, I state it. As I visualize my dream, then I verbalize it by saying, "This is what I believe God wants to do in my life."

Dr. King did this, and it led to immense success.

Publicly stating your dream leads to three effects:

1. It gets you started. There is no more procrastination. Now that I've announced it, I am accountable to make something happen, and I have to get moving.
2. It attracts others' support. The moment I share my dream, others will want to get in on it. A dream from God will attract people you may not know who are willing to help your dream grow.
3. It releases God's power. Because of my faith, I step out of the boat and start walking on water. As long as I stay focused, God will hold me up.

Secure Your Dream

Once we have the dream inside of us, it is the time to secure it. We secure our dreams by seeing where the dream is taking us. To keep our dreams alive, we must write them down and look at them daily. Proverbs 29:18 (NLT) instructs us, "When people do not accept divine guidance, they run wild. But whoever obeys the law is joyful."

Whenever God gives us a dream, He wants to turn our dream into a vision. When it turns into a vision, it will become a reality ... if we work it!

God is a visionary God. He wants to make our dreams a reality. He told an ordinary man to write down what was in his heart so people would be able to understand it. He told Habakkuk in Habakkuk 2:2 (MSG),

> Write this. Write what you see. Write it out in big block letters so that it can be read on the run. This vision-message is a witness pointing to what's coming. It aches for the coming—it can hardly wait! And it doesn't lie. If it seems slow in coming, wait. It's on its way. It will come right on time.

And once my vision is written down, others can see what I want to achieve, which may cause them to join with me and help make the vision a reality. Keep faith, hope, and confidence inside of your dream, which will allow those dreams to remain alive and grow. I have to take control of my dreams and secure them to ensure they flourish and sprout.

As a parent or guardian, we dream about what we want for our children. Normally we dream that they are more successful than what we have become. For them to accomplish this, we must teach them to dream. Often I hear adults tell children, "Stop that daydreaming!" Why? Dreams do not just occur when a person is sleeping; they can happen at any time of the day.

Please do not misunderstand. If a child should focus on their work during school, they must maintain focus to understand their work. Instead when a child is daydreaming, simply ask, "What were you dreaming about?" Once they explain, have them write it or jot it down for them. Then guide them back to the focus of the lesson or task they were working on.

Let them know that what they are daydreaming about can come true if they learn the lesson in front of them. According to Georgia Institute of Technology (Georgia Tech), *Neuropsychologia Journal*, "The team found that people who daydreamed more often also scored higher on tests of intellect and creativity. The MRI results showed that those participants' brains functioned at greater capacity than others."[14] Dreams are dreams whether they occur in the daytime or at night.

Don't crush the dreams of children; instead help to productively nurture them. You may have the next Apple creator or president of the United States sitting at your kitchen table. Our son dreamed of living in Japan, and he has traveled to many countries and experienced more in those four years with the Marines than some people will in a lifetime.

Dream your dream and then pass that legacy to your children so they can fulfill their dreams. Henry Mencken states, "You come into the world with nothing, and the purpose of your life is to make something out of nothing."[15]

> *Securing your dream and then discovering it brings purpose to life.*

Direction 3
Focus Is for Everyone

Every four years, I look forward to watching the Olympics, whether it is the summer or winter games. It is inspirational to watch athletes from around the world focus on their individual disciplines. I watch in awe as they accomplish feats that seem unthinkable for the human body. Regardless of the outcome—whether victory or defeat—I am amazed that they are in the top percentile in their respective sport. As we watch these athletes, many of us receive a burst of inspiration to get active or cultivate a sense of self-doubt that we could never do that. Maybe you wondered, *Could I have that type of focus in my life?*

In case you thought you were alone in being inspired to become more active and go to your local gym after watching the Olympics, you have a lot of company. Research conducted by the Sports & Fitness Industry Association stated, "People tend to show an increased interest in playing sports and being active after watching the Olympics Games ... that year or the next."[16]

The research demonstrates that people find inspiration in others' successes and gifts. We tend to reflect on what-ifs: What if I had taken sports seriously? What if I had listened to the coach? What if I didn't hang out with the guys or girls? What if?

> *This is where self-doubt could enter into the mind. If I had only _____, I would probably _____.*

Only you can fill in those blanks for yourself. However, it is not too late to complete those spaces with positive affirmations. I may not be able to do a particular sport, but I can still find success through the gift within me.

My Purpose and Destiny Are Only a Focus Away

Recently I had to get an eye examination. The doctor moved lenses to various settings until my vision and focus became clear. When I focus, I am seeking a clear sight of my vision. Distractions are the opponent of focus and will take my eyes off the intended target I have set.

Imagine a sprinter running toward the finish line, and about twenty yards away, he suddenly begins to wave at the crowd before getting to the finish line. That sounds absurd, right? If I take my eyes off my target and lose sight of the finish line, I stand a chance of not finishing or losing the race.

That happens to many of us when we begin to focus on a project but then allow distractions to pull us away before reaching the finish line. Martial artist Bruce Lee stated, "The successful warrior is the average man, with laser-like focus."[17] Maintaining focus can be challenging. However, it is achievable if I keep my eyes on the prize I am seeking to obtain.

One Rainy Morning

In the Marine Corps, I had to qualify with the rifle every year. Every Marine is a basic rifleman, and therefore, every Marine, regardless of their MOS, has to qualify and will achieve a rating as a Marksman (the lowest), Sharpshooter (second highest), or Expert (highest level) rifleman.

Focus must be the primary principle of weaponry, or one will not qualify. Shooting, or weaponry, was not a skill I had prior to joining the Corps. During shooting week in boot camp, I could not get the fundamentals. The harder I tried, the worse I shot. Consequently, on qualification day, I did not qualify. That was disappointing, disheartening, and dejecting. My Drill Instructors were not pleased and, in no uncertain terms, made their frustrations known to me.

Later, to my advantage, I had a remedial qualification day, which means I had one more shot (no pun intended) at qualification. If I failed, the Corps would send me to another platoon, which meant I would graduate two weeks later than scheduled.

On requalification day, I struggled with the added pressure. Nevertheless, after my last shot, my Drill Instructor informed me that I had qualified with a score of 190, the qualifying score at that time. I had to push myself not to be distracted while qualifying. It was a liberating feeling to know that I had navigated another obstacle to becoming a United States Marine.

The above scenario is significant because it took me three years to understand the mechanics of shooting correctly. I was missing one—simple—thing, focus. Experienced shooters know that you must focus on the front sight tip of a weapon, without a scope, to hit the target. To become focused, you have to push yourself because most of the time no one is going to push you! I was the only person pushing myself to manipulate that weapon and become an expert shooter. Then one day it happened while serving at Camp LeJeune, North Carolina.

Prior to the practice week, our platoon received a quota for one Marine to go to Sniper School. Our platoon commander challenged us that the highest shooter would get that opportunity. For me, that seemed impossible since I had never shot above a sharpshooter rating. Still during practice week, or what we call grass week (the week of practice shooting), I began to focus like I never had before.

Once practice week was completed, we began the week of pre-qualification and qualification. There are three days of pre-qualification, or practice shooting, and the days began around 5:00 a.m. During the week, I was shooting fairly well, and my confidence increased each day.

The day of qualification occurred on a cold, rainy Thursday morning in March. We finished morning chow and began to assemble in formation to head downrange. If I qualified on Thursday, I was done, but if I did not, remedial qualification would be the next day.

As we stood waiting to go to the shooting line, one of the rifle coaches had a radio playing, and some of the lyrics talked about staying confident and standing your ground.

When I heard these words, something stirred within me. I told myself, "I can do this!" I felt like I had the chance to get the Sniper slot. I began to squash any negative thoughts arising within me. I wanted the Sniper opportunity. My back was against the wall. It was cold and raining, and I knew I could not make any mistakes if I wanted it.

As the qualification started, others in the platoon were saying that another Marine was shooting better than anyone else and that he would get the Sniper slot. He was shooting ahead of me, so I knew what his scores were at each yard line. But I didn't let that distract me. I stayed focused on me.

When I arrived at the 500-yard line, the platoon said his score was 239 (out of a possible 250). I thought to myself, *That is some outstanding shooting!*

Again, I continued to focus on my shooting. I did not keep my score; I did not want to add any more pressure to myself. I knew I had to shoot ten out of ten bull's-eyes to have a chance.

> *I settled in to shoot. I aimed, used my fundamentals, and fired the first shot. Bull's-eye! Second shot. Bull's-eye! Third shot. Bull's-eye!*

Each shot was a perfect bull's-eye. With one shot left, I knew I had to remain calm and stay focused. I used the BRASS system, or

"Breathe, Relax, Aim, Stop, Squeeze. Fire." Some shooters replace the "Stop" with "Slack." Either way, I had to get the correct sight alignment, sight picture for my natural body alignment. I held a six o'clock setting on the sights. The target went down, and when it returned, the result was a bull's-eye!

They relayed and confirmed my score from the target pit. "Corporal Wilder, confirmed score 240 out of a possible 250." I was the highest shooter in the platoon and the fourth-highest shooter on the range that week!

In retrospect, I was not the odds-on favorite to be the highest-scoring shooter. It did not matter. I was the highest-scoring shooter.

The results elicited disbelief from some members in my unit. When you are focused on your goal, you will find critics who want to hamper those goals and dreams. Regardless of the outcome, you have to stay focused on you! During that process, at times I didn't think I could do it, yet I just remained focused on the task ahead of me and blocked out my distractions. I visualized myself going to Sniper School and getting that quota slot. That was the driving force that silenced the noise around me.

Needless to say, becoming the highest-scoring shooter in my platoon that day, getting the quota slot to go to Sniper School, and completing it was one of the one-degree moments for me.

> *Achieving that one act on that cold, rainy day propelled my confidence that I could achieve anything that my heart desired in the Corps.*

I wanted to succeed in everything the Marine Corps had to offer, to live life to the fullest. "A Marine's fighting spirit is their greatest weapon."[18] Even within the greatest fighting force, I had to keep my spirits high, along with a keen sense of focus in order to succeed and take whatever I wanted. I had to allow my spirit to become the weapon that controlled the weapon I was using.

That one-degree moment gave me the confidence to go after other achievements that seemed impossible. A year later, I became a Marine Drill Instructor and served as a Scout Sniper and later still as a Counterintelligence Specialist, where I was able to receive training during Survival, Evasion, Resistance, and Escape (SERE) School, along with other accomplishments.

Reading this book may inspire you to reach for new heights, but that motivation can fade as it meets your day-to-day situations. You may begin to question, "What abilities do I have? I don't have what it takes to be a success."

In the Marine Corps, I was around some of the sharpest warriors in the world, among many that grew up with skills to be a Marine. That was extremely intimidating. Nonetheless, I focused on the skills I had within me and stopped looking at who they were or what they could do. Every now and then, we must focus on ourselves and where we are going in life and then shut out the distractions around us.

Shut Out the Noise

Life can come at us hard, fast, and at breakneck speed. You may experience times where you are jobless, dealing with family issues, in financial despair, or on the verge of retiring. Whatever the case may be, we have to look at the person in the mirror and ask, "What must I do to change my situation?" This may be your one-degree moment as you are scanning these pages. Regardless of the time of day—morning, afternoon, or evening—your new day is beginning right now. Bishop Rick Thomas taught, "Every new day begins at midnight (so don't be afraid to dream in the dark)."[19]

You might be in your midnight hour, and things seem gloomy, but look at how Paul and Silas handled theirs.

> *At midnight Paul and Silas were praying and singing hymns to God, and the prisoners were listening to them. Suddenly there was a great earthquake, so that the foundations of the prison were shaken; and immediately all the doors were opened, and everyone's chains were loosed.*

Acts 16:25–26 (NKJV)

This is the time where you can become free from the situation holding you back from your purpose, from your destiny. No longer will you be bound by the circumstances that are stealing your joy, peace, happiness, and finances! Begin to pray, praise, and believe that you are free from whatever is attempting to hold you from your victory!

Keep in mind that focus is not just for the superstar athlete, the prominent business owner, or the successful doctor or lawyer. Focus is for anyone who desires in their heart to be a better person. It is as simple as writing down what you want or see it for yourself. I shared earlier from Habakkuk 2:2 (NLT), "Then the Lord said to me, 'Write my answer plainly on tablets, so that a runner can carry the correct message to others.'"

We must write our vision, what do we see ourselves doing, and then turn that vision into goals (achievable steps). Share the vision with our mentors and those who can join with us so they can carry our message to other visionaries.

When our vision is carried out, someone could be looking for what we are seeking, which could be the opportunity for our visions and dreams to come alive. Be prepared for an opportunity. It could be just around the corner from you.

> *When an idea or thought comes to mind, write it down.*
> *It might not be for today, it could be for something*
> *coming a year from now, just write it down.*

We all have smartphones that have a notepad app. Instead of using your phone to watch a video, play a game, or just listen to music, use it to write your vision. Writing down your dreams, visions, and goals allows you to get prepared for the opportunity that is just around the corner.

I have read historical and modern-day testimonies of others who have had one-degree moments. As I read them, I think about how fortunate they were to get that break.

We often see the end of their journey, but not what it took or the work they had to put in for them to reach success:

- Dr. Martin Luther King Jr.'s moment came as a result of Rosa Parks refusing to give up her bus seat on December 1, 1955, which launched the Civil Rights Movement.
- Stephen Hawking, the brilliant mind behind general relativity and quantum gravity, came in a 1965 lecture.
- World-renowned pastor, the late Dr. Myles Munroe, had his turning point as a teen when he was told he would not be successful.

Each of them had to shut out the noise to allow them to let their dreams come alive. And parents, when the system gives up on your child, continue to pour into their life to allow the dreams inside of them to grow. Teach your children and the younger generation to dream. Coach them on how to write down their dreams, visions, and goals.

> *When my children were younger, I would say to them,*
> *"You are leaders; you were designed to be successful."*

I did not stop when they became adults. I continue to send them motivational quotes, sayings, or videos to remind them to stay focused on their purpose and destiny. I tell them often to write down what they see, where they envision themselves going, or what they desire. When our hope is delayed, it can make us feel depressed, but when desire is achieved, it comes alive!

We all need that affirmation because life will constantly remind us that we are not the success that God intended for us to have in our lives. Abraham Lincoln commented, "In the end, it's not the years in your life that count. It's the life in your years."[20]

Life doesn't always just come at us hard; it sometimes just runs us over! When that happens, we have to remain focused and keep looking at our dreams, visions, and goals to remind us that our success is one prayer away. Continue to shower your children with positive declarations. Those words can trigger a one-degree moment in their lives to help them unleash their focus and bring them immense success.

Direction 4
One-Degree Moments

Dale Carnegie said, "Remember, today is the tomorrow you worried about yesterday."[21] We cannot dwell on the past or worry about tomorrow. We remember the past but don't focus on it, and we look out for tomorrow but don't get consumed with it. We have to focus on today, which has its own issues to tangle with.

Stay focused on what is in front of you. One degree
off your mark could make you miss your destination.

Neil Anderson states, "When you live in a constant state of anxiety, most of life passes you by because you are physically, emotionally and mentally unable to focus on the fear that is swallowing you."[22] Remember the acronym for FEAR: False—Evidence—Appearing—Real. Fear can blind us if we are one-degree off our mark.

On the opposite side, the Bible tells us that faith is the confidence of things that we hope to receive and the declaration regarding things we are not able to see. (See Hebrews 11:1.) When we have the faith to believe, it will cancel out the fear.

As I wrote this book, I reached out to some friends and asked if they would share their one-degree testimonies. Each of them canceled out fear of the past and allowed faith to direct their future. During their younger years, they were headed in wrong directions and did some things that could have changed the course of their lives and landed them many degrees away from their set destination. Some of it dealt with fear; others involved misguided faith.

As you will read, God's mercy allowed them to share their stories from their current positions rather from a jail cell or someone else telling their story because they were no longer here. Here are their one-degree moments in their own words.

Rese Jackson, Associate Minister and Lighting Technician Specialist

Rese was born in Sanford, Florida, in 1979. He grew up with both parents in a church-connected house. He said, "My dad only went to church for weddings and funerals up to the year 2005 when I led him to the Lord through salvation with Jesus Christ." His mother though was in church every Sunday. During the week, church was not the topic in his house. He stated that his family had a form of religion, a fear-based one, but not a personal relationship with Jesus Christ.

Rese and his family moved from Central Florida to Deerfield Beach in South Florida. His parents tried to get him back into church, but he was not interested in the church scene. He stated, "I prayed religiously when things went wrong, but it was not a relationship type of prayer. I believed in the existence of Christ, but not enough for a relationship with Him. I did not step back into a church until I was twenty-one years old."

As we continued to talk, the conversation shifted to the topic of influence. The biggest influence in his early years was his father. Then we spoke about his one-degree moment. Rese, in his own words, told the following story.

> Although we did not attend church, I was exposed to drugs and alcohol, but I was not allowed to touch any of it. If I tried to, I would have found myself in trouble. The reason for their attitude is that my people viewed me as the one who would make it out of this lifestyle.
>
> Even though I was told to avoid it, I had to be sneaky and play both sides of the fence. I knew if I were caught with it, it could get me hurt. I knew

this was not something I should be doing, and I knew I could get taken out for messing with drugs. Of course, this was not based on the influence I had or was exposed to or the role models who were present in my life.

Playing Both Sides of the Fence

Unfortunately at the age of fourteen, a shift in the family pushed me deeper into the drug culture. Our family became a one-income family. It changed my lifestyle, which forced me to peddle drugs a little harder. I began selling at the age of fourteen and continued through my high school years. I somewhat felt that my family had an idea of what I was doing, but no one ever mentioned it to me.

While in high school, I was working at a fast-food joint and national retail store, and I was paying the bills in the household. No way can those two jobs pay for that. All the while, I played football and basketball and was involved in the Junior Reserve Officers' Training Corps (JROTC) at school.

Although I had this secret lifestyle, my plan was, if the football thing didn't work, I would go into the military. In fact, I received a scholarship to play basketball, but I knew college was not the way I wanted to go. Plus, I was making big money with my hidden trade.

Meanwhile, I was set to go to the Marine Corps after graduation, but while I was waiting, my brother got me a part-time job working at the local stage theatre, cleaning, mopping, and so forth. I didn't care because my party life was off the chain. I was making runs with the drugs to different cities up and down the East Coast. I was living life.

I was ready to go to the Marines, but my mom was really leery about it. She said, "I don't think you should go to the Marines!" I told her I was already signed up and had to go. The day after that conversation, I received a call from the boss at the theatre, asking me to work a show. I did and made $500. Prior to that, I was making $135 a week.

I asked him, "How much money can I make doing this?"

He tossed me a book called *Lighting for Dummies* and said, "Read this and you can make eighty thousand per year."

I then called the Marine Recruiter, and due to some issues with my medical record, my contract was voided out. I didn't know it then, but God had a different plan for my life. A week later, one of the stage managers offered me a full-time position with the theatre, the first African American working full time with the theatre. I was only eighteen years old doing all of this.

One-Degree Moment: On the Side of the Road

About eighteen months later, life was good. I was running drugs with a pocket full of money, and I met a young lady who invited me to live in New York. I agreed to go. I told my drug boss that I was leaving to go up North, and he told me, "I got a load for you to carry." This was the largest load I had ever carried, about $216,000 of narcotics.

About two weeks before I was to leave, a good friend invited me to a party with the stipulation that if we went, I had to go to church with him the next morning. So we went, and true to his word, the next morning we went to Abundant Life Christian Center in Margate, Florida. After hearing Pastor Rick Thomas' sermon, something began to stir in me.

The day arrived for me to go to New York. My mom told me, crying, she did not feel good about this journey. This was not normal for me, as my mom did not cry. I left for my trip and stopped in South Carolina to see my grandmother.

At breakfast, my grandmother told me, "God has a calling on your life, and some people answer the call hard."

I was not sure what she was talking about. Not long after leaving her house, I was involved in an eight-car wreck in North Carolina. The drugs were all over the ground, people could see them, and all I could think was, *My life is over, and I will go to prison for the rest of my life.*

I said, "Lord, what my grandma just said to me, I could use that right now. If you get me out of this, I will never do this stuff again."

I looked to my left saw and the officer coming. I looked to my right and observed a flatbed truck that looked like it was for me. I made a deal with the tow truck driver, and he agreed to take my car. I scooped up the drugs and threw the clothes over it.

The officer took statements from everyone, ticketed the other guy, asked if that were my flatbed, and told me to appear in court if I wanted to testify. The tow truck driver took me to a rundown motel.

While I was there, I read a Gideon Bible laying on the nightstand. I had not read the Bible since I was nine years old. The next day I got a rental car, completed my trip to New York, dropped off the stuff, and continued to party.

About nine months later, I returned to South Florida for my dad's birthday in December. I was at my aunt's house, and I called one of the guys and told him, "I'm home if you need me to make a run." As was the norm, he told me there was a load for the west coast of Florida. Three days went by, and I didn't hear from the guy.

One day I was by myself in the house, and I flipped on the television. A Christian program came on. I paused it on the station, and this is where the one-degree came to life.

The pastor on television said, "I normally don't end my broadcast this way, but a young man listening who eight months earlier made a deal with the Lord, and you are about to do something. If you go through with it, you will never see the light of day as a free man."

I was now weeping. It didn't get any clearer than that. I prayed the prayer of salvation with the pastor on television, and I knew I had to go back to church. That was a Saturday.

The next day, I returned to Abundant Life and gave my life to the Lord that morning with Pastor Rick leading the prayer. I was the only one to come forward, and he told the congregation, "Do you see this young man? I don't know him, but God's hand is upon him. He is going to do something great for God, so don't ever let him feel alone."

Since that day, I have probably missed only ten Sundays, and now God is using me for the kingdom.

Rese is now an ordained minister at Abundant Life Church under the leadership of Bishop Rick Thomas. He has served in myriad positions since giving his life to Christ. He served as the youth pastor for several years and in local high school ministries, and churches around the country seek his services to set up their sound and lighting. He was the lead technician to set up the sound and lighting for a new building for Abundant Life Church. He mentors young men on how to discover their life's purpose and was instrumental in helping his wife, Jenya, with her debut album, *Conquerors*.

Martha Savloff, Minister and Entrepreneur

"It was an eerie afternoon when my life changed," Martha said. Martha was born and raised in a large Spanish-speaking family near the Flagler area of Miami, Florida. She grew up with her parents and sister. Her stay-at-home mom had little trade or work skills; her late dad had an entrepreneurial spirit and tried all the get-rich-quick schemes to support the family. He owned multiple businesses.

The family had a great life and did not want for anything, as Martha's dad provided everything they wanted, but her family did not go to church. Martha said, "We only attended church for weddings and baptisms." Her parents believed that God existed, but they were not active with the church. Martha explained that the church had hurt them when she was a child.

"My sister and I were to be baptized, and we had a little bit of money to present. It wasn't a lot, but the priest actually counted it in front of us and said it was not enough. He rejected our offering and us from being baptized. Since then we had never gone back to church until later in life."

From Riches to Rags

Martha, in her own words, told the following story.

> When I was around fifteen years old on a quiet, eerie afternoon, my family and I came home to find that my dad had literally kicked us out of the house. I didn't understand what was happening, except we had nowhere to go. At that moment, we went literally from riches to rags. He put us out with nothing—no car, no clothes, nothing. I remember this like it was yesterday.
>
> We lived in the Flagler area, and most of my family lived in the Hialeah area, about fifteen to twenty miles away.
>
> I really resented my dad and thought he was a horrible man. As I got older, I found out that some indiscretions happening on both parts led to his putting us out. Actually things were happening with both my parents. My mom was my dad's fourth marriage, and there were some lifestyle differences.

At that moment, so many emotions were going through my head. What was going to happen to us? Where would we live? Would I graduate from high school? How could he do this to us? I was a wreck, but one thing I said to myself as we were walking away from the house, "I will never put myself in this type of situation. I will never depend on a man."

Mom was now a single mom with no career, trade, or education (at the time), no nothing, and now we were walking away with nothing. She got a job in a lab and later took a job at Dunkin' Donuts. We eventually found a bug-infested apartment. Every night I felt things crawling all over my legs as I tried to sleep. It was definitely not the best conditions for us, but again we had to make the most of what we had at that time.

Seeing what happened to my mom caused me to have anger issues and to put up a wall to never trust anyone or allow myself to be put in a situation like she experienced. This incident caused me to become an overachiever in everything I did out of fear of being in that type of circumstance. Of course, this caused a strain on the relationship I had with my dad.

Losing What I Loved

I went to South Miami High School, where I was a great student in arts and dance classes, but I didn't care about math, English, and science. However, my sister was an Advanced Placement student, and my dad would favor her. He consistently did things that would remind me that I was not an academically sharp student.

For instance, he would put things on the table to see how long it would take me to pick it up or remove it, and if it took a long time, he would yell and scream at me. He was literally setting me up to make me feel inadequate. One time while I was still in high school, he wanted dinner at a certain time, and I was about two minutes late getting it to the table. He took the plate and threw it on the floor, and when it broke, a piece hit my forehead and cut me. This made me really resent my dad and how he treated me. Our relationship was not good because of all the things he put me through. I did not let it spoil my love for the arts, specifically dance.

As I was getting close to graduation, I received a scholarship to the University of Miami for dance. Unfortunately I never accepted it or went to the university because of my family situation. Instead I worked to help support the family. A little later, I went to Miami Dade College but only took a couple of classes. I never completed college.

Because I lost my scholarship due to the circumstances that my dad put us through and what I had to endure from him, I developed anger and daddy issues. In high school, I also dealt with being bullied, enduring an attempted rape, and having to work to help support the family.

I carried this anger with me. If you messed with me, I would just fight you with no hesitation. One guy would bully me every day about the same time, and one day he put whipped cream on some expensive shorts that my mom had bought me. I snapped! I was so upset because my mom had worked endless hours to afford these shorts. I beat him down, and after that, people knew I would fight them at the drop of a dime.

I was still involved in various organizations, such as the treasurer for the dance club and the student body government. I could not do a lot with other activities because I helped my mom by working after school as well.

I had no clue or direction of what I wanted to do. I was just going to school, working, partying, and letting life pass me by. But even with a lack of direction, I always maintained a great work ethic. My first real job was at a movie theater. I was determined not to put myself in the same situation I had experienced. That experience gave me the drive not to be placed in that type of circumstance ever!

Meeting at the Copying Machine

After graduation and with my scholarship gone, I continued to focus on work. I got a job with a temp agency, which assigned me to an insurance company. One day I had to make some copies, and the machine in my department was not working. I went to the finance department. A man came over and asked if he could make one copy. My anger issues rose up, and I told him no, saying that he had to wait. I eventually let him make his one copy.

About three months later, I heard through coworkers that this man was telling people that he liked me. One day I sent him a rose and invited him out to lunch. He showed with five of his friends, and to impress me, he paid for everyone. That man was Gus, who became my husband. Later in our relationship, I found out that he had told his mom that he had found his future wife after the copying machine incident.

Since that first lunch, we have been together. Eleven months later, Gus and I married. Just like any couple, we were excited about spending our lives together; however, the anger issues still lingered in my life, and we had heated arguments. It seemed that we fought about everything.

Although we were married, our lifestyle did not change. We were still partying, drinking, and living like we were prior to marriage.

One Degree: The Journey with Gus

We moved to the Cape Coral, Florida, area, but Gus's job was in Sunrise, Florida, just over two hours away. We had been married just over five years with two small children. His office was on the second floor of a building; the first floor was a small Caribbean church led by Pastor Prophet Jeremiah, a tall, robust man.

Whenever Prophet Jeremiah saw Gus in the parking lot, he would stop and talk to him. Of course, Gus did not want to hear anything about church. Both of us were not into the church thing, and we never attended services.

One year Gus and I decided to spend Thanksgiving with family in Miami. Upon returning home, we found our house had been ransacked. Someone had come in and destroyed everything—our television, furniture, personal items, everything! It didn't look like they had stolen anything, but it was a vicious personal attack. We suspected who might have done it, but we could not prove anything.

We were devastated. We did not have any money. We were living from paycheck to paycheck. We had to roll pennies to get food at times. Having our place destroyed set us back a lot.

While we did not go to church or want anything to do with church, the Sunday following the destruction of our home, Gus announced, "We are going to church." We drove two and half hours to Prophet Jeremiah's church in Sunrise. When we walked in, casually dressed, and everyone else was dressed nicely. Men were in their suits; ladies had on hats. It was very nice.

When Prophet Jeremiah saw us enter, he exclaimed, "Gus! I knew you were coming today! Stop the service! I knew you were coming!"

During the service, Prophet Jeremiah called us to come forward and began to prophesy over us. I was shaking because I had never experienced anything like this. He prophesied over Gus. Then he came to me. He told me about an injury to my shoulder that no one knew about. He began to describe things in our house, even the color of our tile. It was mind-blowing.

He continued to pray over us. Then he gave me a dollar and told us it would be the best Christmas of our lives. He then said, "When you leave the service, you are going to get a call. You are not only going to get one check. You are going to get two!"

This was hard to believe, especially considering that our house had been destroyed and we did not have any money. But that day we both accepted Jesus Christ in our lives with Prophet Jeremiah.

We walked out of the church and were sitting in the car in the parking lot, stunned at what had just happened before driving off. Gus's phone rang, and it was a man who owed Gus some money. The man said, "I left two checks for you at the guardhouse of my apartment. Cash one on Monday and the other on Wednesday." We were in total shock!

This was new to us, so we called my mother-in-law to have her explain what we just experienced. We were silent on the drive back home.

The following Monday, Gus said, "Let's go get a Christmas tree."

My anger issues reared up again, and I yelled, "A Christmas tree! We don't have any money! How are we going to get a tree with no money?"

Gus didn't stop. He said, "Let's go to the store and get a tree."

Again, I yelled at him and told him that the store was too expensive. But I gave in, and we went to the store to get a tree.

When we arrived, I saw a beautiful, tall tree, and I was looking up at it in awe.

Gus came over and asked, "Do you want me to ask how much?"

"That tree won't cost twenty dollars." That was our tree budget.

An employee approached us and inquired, "Do you like that tree? It was sent to us by mistake, and if you have twenty dollars, you can take it."

I was blown away at what was happening to us over the course of two days!

The following day, I went to work and found a gift on my desk, a box of tree decorations. My coworkers did not know that I had bought a tree or did not have decorations, but they had decided to buy this for me. At that point, we knew something miraculous was happening in our lives. After that experience with God, we were in church every Sunday.

We made the two-and-a-half-hour drive to Prophet Jeremiah's church every Sunday for over four months. One Sunday, Prophet Jeremiah told us that we needed to find a local church to attend because this was too far for us to be driving every week. We eventually found a church in our area,

Fort Myers Christian Outreach Center, under the leadership of Pastor Lynn Braco.

As a new Christian, I was a work-in-progress. My anger issues continued, but I was working on them. During a service, I was asked if my daughter could be in one of the children's programs. While I was waiting for her to finish practice one day, another mother began to talk to me and asked about my life. I told her a little about my life as a dancer.

She immediately shared that information with one of the pastors of the church, who asked if I could dance at the church on Friday. It was Tuesday when she asked me to dance. I was in shock! I did not know you could dance in church.

From that point, I was in dance ministry with the church, and I have never looked back. That one moment with Prophet Jeremiah was my one-degree moment that changed my entire life. The pastor at Christian Outreach became my mentor, and through her counsel, I was able to deal with my anger issues and learn how to forgive. I know that God has chosen me to do His work.

Martha continued to share about her life with me, explaining that through her transformation with Christ and through the Word of God, she discovered that she is truly chosen. Her favorite scripture is found in John 15:16 (NKJV), "You did not choose me, but I chose you and appointed you so that you might go and bear fruit." This has become a scripture she lives by and shares with others.

Martha is an ordained minister who has served at Fort Myers Christian Outreach Center in dance and leadership roles, and she was the Director of the Dance Ministry at Abundant Life Church in Margate, Florida, where she titled the ministry "Chosen" from Acts 17:28. She currently attends New Wine Ministries in Cooper City, Florida.

Martha and I discussed how forgiveness grew out of her transformed heart. She forgave her dad after attending an Abundant Life retreat weekend. She continued, "God gave me a heart of compassion toward my father. It was like I had gone through a heart transplant. I had a revelation at that moment that hurt people really do hurt people. At that time, my dad was dealing with hard times with his business and his own personal struggles. After everything, I honor my dad, and I love him immensely!"

Her spiritual heart transplant allowed her to heal from the pains of the past. She concluded, "I have so much gratitude in my heart due to my struggles and where God has taken me because through Him, I am chosen."

Martha is the owner/operator of Inspire Weight Loss & Health Coaching (www.inspire-weightloss.com), a business she believes that God has chosen her to accomplish.

D. W., Retired Military Officer and Businessman/Mentor

Born and raised in the Tallahassee area, Florida, with both his mom, late dad, and brothers and sisters, D. W. is a graduate of Leon County Public School System, where he played football. He grew up in a disciplinarian home. He shared, "My mom was more of the disciplinarian, and my dad was more of an introvert who led by example."

D. W. grew up going to church, stating that his mom ensured that they went to church every Sunday. His grandfather was the biggest influence in his life. He said, "My granddad was always around, a real talkative man and a very outspoken person who shaped my personality into the person I am today. I learned a lot from my dad too, but my character of who I am came from my granddad."

Like many young people, although he had positive influences around him, an element pushed him to the other side of the realm. Here's his one-degree story in his own words.

> When I was in middle school, I met this group of guys. There were four of us who seemed to be the popular guys at that moment. They were not the best influence, but over time we bonded. They became a big influence on me, even greater than my parents. I began to hang around them, and I soon struggled with doing the right thing, which had been taught to me at home, or choosing to go in a negative direction. I struggled to choose between the two, but peer pressure got the better of me, and I chose the wrong path.
>
> *One Bullet Makes a Difference*
>
> We were not into any hardcore things, but we were doing illegal things. For instance, we would fight, shoplift and commit petty thefts, and do mild drugs, just things like that. One guy was like the ringleader. He was a little older, I think about two or three years older than the rest of us, and he had the most influence over us.
>
> I knew that this was not the direction I was supposed to go, but I felt like I was with the right gang. As we grew older, we began to do more and more illegal things and were heading straight toward a criminal lifestyle. In fact, one of the guys hurt someone and was sent to a reform school for about a year. When

he returned, he was placed back in regular school. He thought he should be the leader now because he had earned his "stripes" in jail.

With his street cred backing us, we escalated to carrying knives, brass knuckles, and even guns. I carried an illegal .38 snub-nosed pistol with me. This was not a good thing for me to have, but I was a part of the gang.

In my senior year, we were at a park and had some words with a rival gang of guys from town. While we were arguing with them, one of the rival guys threw a blindside punch and hit our gang leader, who, knowing I had the gun, yelled at me, "Shoot, shoot, shoot 'em!"

I pulled the gun out of my waistband, and without thinking, just being young and dumb, I started shooting. I had never shot a gun before in my life and had no clue what I was doing.

A lot of people were at the park, and everyone ran and ducked behind things. I fired all five rounds, and by the grace of God, no one was hit. I put the gun in my waistband, and we got in the car and drove off. Within minutes, the police were everywhere. I don't know where all these police came from, but there they were. They stopped the car, arrested all of us, and took us to jail. As a juvenile, I was assigned a Juvenile Parole Officer (JPO) while I waited for my court hearing.

One-Degree Moment: The Judge

When I went before the judge, my parents were with me. The judge noticed that I had never been in trouble before. All of the other guys had juvenile records.

The judge said, "I think you are salvageable. You come from a good family, and I feel you were under peer pressure. I looked at your grades and conduct in school and think you are worth saving. I tell you what, young man. I will drop all the charges if you join the armed forces."

I replied, "Armed forces?"

I did not know anything about the armed forces, except for an older family member who had been in Vietnam. The judge gave me a few days to think it over. I talked to my family member who was in the Army, and he advised, "Maybe you should consider the military."

I talked to my parents, and they thought this might be a good opportunity for me to get out of town and do something positive. I went back to the judge and told him that I would join the military. I was assigned a recruiter, took the test, and passed, and now the rest is history.

D. W.'s story, like many others, had that one-degree moment where one bullet could have changed his life. If one of those bullets had struck someone or even killed a person, we would not be having this conversation. If the judge had not been merciful and given D. W. another chance, we would not be having this discussion.

However, because of that one-degree moment, D. W. went on to have a successful, thirty-year career in the military. He earned his master's degree in marketing, owned a retail clothing business, and has several homes and cars to his credit, and now he gives back by mentoring young males within a mentoring group.

D. W. said, "I want to reach back and assist these young males before they head in a negative direction in life." He gives the benefit of his wisdom, life experiences, and a helping hand to these young males.

Ramon "Absoloot" Robinson, National Recording Artist, Best-Selling Author, and Entrepreneur

Born in Clearlake in Northern California and raised in Broward County, Florida, Ramon "Absoloot" Robinson is making his mark in society. He is an independent artist, activist, musician, entertainer, and author. However, his beginnings were humble. Ramon grew up in a two-parent home. His family was involved in community outreach and giving back. He is the youngest of five siblings. Ramon has a good relationship with his siblings. His nephew, who stayed with Ramon's family, was the catalyst for his one-degree moment.

In Ramon's younger years, the influence of church came through his grandmother in Texas, as he had visited her during summer vacations. This influence impacted his life and, as he attested, made him the person he is today.

During his middle school years, Ramon went to a religious school where he had a bad experience with the Headmaster/Principal. It also left a bad perception of the church with him until he ultimately did not want anything more to do with it. Since then, he has matured in understanding that the church was not bad, just the person he dealt with. He explained that he now has an amazing relationship with God and gives Him the glory daily for his blessings.

In high school, Ramon was not sure about his future or where he wanted to go. He knew he wanted to do music or comics but was told there was not a career in either. However, he kept his focus and mind on doing both. Even with the bad experience about church, Ramon believed that God had a plan for his life involving music.

A variety of people were positive influences in his life, although the principal was not. Ramon continued to feel the urge to listen to music, regardless of what others stated that he could or could not do with it.

Ramon's Story: It Was Scary Not Doing Music

Ramon shared the following story about himself.

> Coming out of high school, I did not see myself doing anything but music and comic books. These two things kept me going. The bad experiences in middle school and being told that I could not make a career with music or comic books literally scared me. I knew I did not want to work for anyone, but the thought of not being able to do these two passions almost made me depressed.
>
> Even though I was not in church at the time, I knew that God had something greater for me, but how was I going to do it? I did not know what I was going to be or do because so many people told me it was not possible.
>
> This attitude carried over from high school into college. While in college at Johnson and Wales in Providence, Rhode Island, I felt out of place. I played basketball there and was pretty good, but I knew there was something greater for me. God was showing me that music and comics were the things for me and He would not let me rest.

I left after a year in college, and it wasn't until I was twenty-six that everything started to unfold. Even when I worked other jobs, I would listen to music, not for the entertainment, but to see how it was broken down, how they layered the tracks or arranged the sounds. Music can lead you down a path, but which path is the right one?

At twenty-three, I signed a record deal. The type of music I was doing was not me, but I had a record deal. The first album was called *Raw*. I was around a group of guys who were into all kinds of things. Here I was, riding around in Bentleys and Mercedes and wearing $25,000 chains and a $15,000 watch.

I was in the Wisconsin area, riding in a Bentley with a group of other expensive cars. I'm not sure what section of the city we were in, but it was an impoverished area. As we were riding, a car began to follow us. I told my friend who was driving, "A truck is following us."

The driver called the other cars that were with us and told our group what was going on. When we stopped, the guys in the truck came out with guns. We had security with us, and security got out of their cars and showed their weapons. The guys in the truck jumped back in and left.

This made me realize that flashing jewelry and riding around in expensive cars in a low-income area was setting us up for disaster. I could have been robbed or even killed over some inanimate objects. What was the purpose of me doing that? I came from a background of helping people, and now I was flashing signals to people who looked like me but did not have much. I felt horrible making people feel as though they were less than myself.

Unfortunately, my perceived notion of success was really a façade. This was what others wanted me to believe was success. Now, here is where life gets interesting. When we were in the Wisconsin area, I noticed a white Cadillac Escalade had been following us through the cities we had been traveling to. I did not know this at the time, but one of the main investors for the record label, a close family friend, was arrested. He had been selling drugs, and a lot of the money for the label was coming from the drug money.

One day he called me up and said, "Mon [He called me Mon, short for Ramon], hey, I need to meet with you."

I asked, "What's up? What's going on?"

"Man, I messed up. I messed up bad."

I met him at a fast-food restaurant, and when I got there, the place was packed with unmarked police cars.

I asked, "Man, what is going on?"

He replied, "They got me, man. They got me."

After I met with him, the police came back to my house and took stuff from there, and then we went to my parents' mortgage business. My parents let us use one of their offices as a studio. The police took all the equipment, computers, cars, jewelry, everything. I did not sell any drugs or do anything illegal, but because I was associated with him, I was guilty by association. I was not arrested, but I lost everything material that day.

I became depressed, so my parents told me to come back home and stay with them until everything calmed down. Here I was, at a moment, going from a lavish lifestyle to having nothing, staying at home with my parents. This was not where I had seen my life leading me. But believe it or not, even with the pain and hurt of losing everything, this was not my one-degree moment.

One-Degree Moment: When a Child Sings a Song

During this time, I went to visit my sister at her church. She and her husband, both pastors, were doing great work in the community with feeding and clothing programs. That Sunday, I attended church with them. One of my younger nephews, who was around five or six years old at the time, was hanging out with me in the back of the church. I loved this boy so much. During the service, he began to sing one of my songs, a negative tune called "Hustles & Hoes." I was shocked that he was singing this song at such a young age!

Right at that moment, I thought to myself, *Through all the things I have seen and been through—the people and friends I have lost through death—if I give my nephew the impression that what I am doing is cool and I lose him from something that I said through these lyrics, everything he does based around that music, that is all on me. If he thought that talking about women in a degrading way or people in a negative way, that came from me!*

At that moment, I said, "I will never curse on another record. I will never use a derogatory word again because I would never give him the impression that was cool. From that moment, I have never used profanity or degraded anyone through my music!"

God spoke to me as I witnessed this and said, "Look at this. This is your message coming through your nephew! He is saying what you said!"

As I observed this through my nephew, I got emotional. As time went on, I reflected on the power of words through music. As I mentioned, I lost a lot of friends through tragedy, from this negative time in life that I was leading. That one-degree moment propelled me to see life positively and know that God has and had a better plan for me. Through all the ups and downs I have experienced, knowing that my words have an impact on others' lives made me realize that being positive can inspire others to become great in their lives. I choose to inspire rather than destroy.

Since this one-degree moment, Ramon has been successful with various projects. God has elevated him to new heights since having a positive persuasion. In 2009, he was invited to the Grammys for his album, *My Way.* His popularity grew. He had over 23 million streams and acquired more than 100,000 followers through social media. With his song "99 Percent," *The Huffington Post* featured his song for the Occupy Wall Street Movement. Additionally, his comic books have received bestseller status, and they have been selected to be read in the Broward County School District.

Ramon is a mentor with Men2Boys Mentoring Group. He is genuine and authentic, and what he shares with audiences, either adults or children, makes him the "Absoloot" truth.

These life stories may seem extreme, and you might be saying, "I have not done anything that harsh or placed myself in these situations." However, when you reflect on your life, take a look at how close you could have come to altering your destiny. With each one of these testimonies, you can see how God showed mercy, and through His mercy, God's empowering presence, His grace was with them.

The stories were designed to let you know that each of us, regardless of degree or condition, could find ourselves headed in the wrong direction. God's mercy keeps us from going too far away from what He had planned for our lives.

Jimmy Dean, the American country singer and founder of Jimmy Dean Sausage, said it best, "I can't change the direction of the wind, but I can adjust my sails to always reach my destination."[23] We may not be able to control the circumstances around us but know that we are in control of our own destiny through God's grace.

When faced with life choices, always ensure that you are navigating in the direction that God intended for you to travel. The people who told their stories took a hold of the sails of life and allowed God to be the air in their sails and push them in the right direction for success.

> *You have the same opportunity to grab a hold of life. Let God be the wind and then set your sails for success!*

Direction 5
Prayer Changes Things

In the opening direction, I mentioned how I met one of the meanest individuals on the planet, the Marine Drill Instructor. Just over six years after joining the Corps, I had the opportunity to be on the other side of the yelling. I became a Marine Drill Instructor at Marine Corps Recruit Depot, San Diego, California, with the 1st Recruit Training Battalion, Company C (Charlie Company).

Serving as a Drill Instructor is an arduous task. Drill Instructors are charged with producing the finest war fighters that the world has ever seen. Tremendous stress is placed on us. Our reputation is on the line if we produce anything less than the best. My time as a Drill Instructor was no exception. Let me take you to boot camp.

Right Place, Wrong Time

When I was assigned to Charlie Company, I immersed myself in training the recruits. I worked at becoming the meanest Drill Instructor in order to produce the best recruits for the Corps. My training platoons were successful, and I felt I was doing what I was trained to do, produce the best. We had won various drill competitions and academic awards along with best scores as a platoon for rifle qualification.

Then it happened. I was a few months shy of a full tour and ready to be promoted to Senior Drill Instructor (in charge of the platoon). As I was training my fifth platoon, we were midway through the training cycle when I was summoned from the rifle range to the company's First Sergeant's office.

I arrived at his office. He said, "Come in Sergeant Wilder. Stand at ease. Hey Marine, you have allegations stating that you were aware of recruits attacking another recruit."

"What? Are you serious First Sergeant?! I was not aware of anything like that!"

"I understand what you are saying Sergeant Wilder, however, these are the allegation and I am going to have to read you your 'Miranda Rights' so that you understand that anything you say after that can be used against you."

"Read me the 'Miranda Rights?! "First Sergeant, you are kidding me, right?! This is not right. I was not aware of that and I did not issue any such order to my platoon!"

"I believe what you are saying, but these are the allegations against you."

(After reading the 'Miranda Rights') "Sergeant Wilder, you are suspended from the training platoon until further notice. Give me your campaign cover (Drill Instructor hat) and your duty belt. Go home and wait for my call for the next step in the process."

With shock I responded, "Aye, Aye, First Sergeant, but this is not right!!"

"You are dismissed Sergeant Wilder."

To have to give up your campaign cover and duty belt and wait for a phone call with the outcome is one of the worst feelings a Drill Instructor can experience.

During the drive home, I was devastated with what had just transpired in the First Sergeant's office. I was thinking, "How would I explain this to my wife? How will she handle it? What was going to happen to me? Why is this happening to me!" My mind was swimming with all kinds of thoughts.

When I arrived at our apartment, getting out my car and walking to the door seem to take forever. When I entered the apartment, I spoke to my wife, and she immediately knew something was not right. I walked into the bedroom, sat on the edge of the bed, placed my face in my hands with tearful eyes, and began to explain to her what happened.

"Baby, they just said that I am suspended from work pending an investigation of some of the recruits attacking other recruits and that I was responsible for it!"

She said, "Do they have any proof that you did anything?"

"No! Just the allegations that I allegedly knew they were attacking other recruits. What they are saying about me is not true! I didn't do anything like that!"

With tears in her eyes, she grabbed my hands and said, "Honey, let's pray! We will get through this!"

Once she completed the prayer, I laid on the bed in agony over this entire ordeal.

She said, "we will get through this. You have to believe that!"

"Okay baby! I believe we will!" Although I was thinking would I get through it?

A week later, I received a call to report to the First Sergeant's office. When I walked in, two other senior Marines were present as witnesses. My heart sank. I knew it wasn't going to be good.

"Sergeant Wilder reporting as ordered First Sergeant."

"Stand at ease. Sergeant Wilder, you are being charged with the allegations against you. Do you have any questions before I continue?"

"No First Sergeant."

He began to read me my Miranda Rights again and the informal charges. Upon completion of this process, he told me to report to the battalion Sergeant Major's office. I was in shock at what was happening. After reporting to the Sergeant Major's office, he escorted me to the battalion Executive Officer's office, where the charges against me were officially read.

Eight charges were read against me, and I was informed that I was going before a special court-martial trial. The severity of this type of court, at that time, along with the charges, could result in a thirty-month confinement (jail), reduction in rank, and forfeiture of my pay.

Needless to say, this was devastating, not just for me, but for my wife as well, and she continued to pray about it. Though I was not into prayer then, I felt she needed some help, so I called my parents, my wife's mom, and my grandparents. I needed some heavy artillery prayers with this situation.

Nearly three weeks had passed, and a court-martial date was set. The Marine Corps assigned lawyers to represent me; however, I was able to hire a civilian attorney instead who happened to be a retired Marine Corps Colonel and former military attorney. He prepared me for the onslaught I was about to face.

The court-martial began about two months later. It was a pleasant October morning, but to me it was oppressively overcast. The opening arguments began, and the prosecutor painted a picture of me that seemed to set my fate right out of the gate. You could hear gasps in the courtroom, as if I were guilty before the trial had even begun. I was in disbelief that this was actually happening.

All the while, my wife and family were praying for me. During the grueling three-day trial, I was emotionally and physically exhausted. My lawyer was amazing, as he counterpunched everything the prosecutor was throwing at me. The trial was on its last day, and my fate seemed bleak, at least from my perspective. Right when I thought it was over, it happened.

Mercy Said "Step Aside"

Woodrow Kroll said, "Justice is for those who deserve it, mercy is for those who don't."[24] The Marine Corps expects Drill Instructors to be tough, mean, and hard on the recruits; however, they expect it to be done within the set rules and guidelines. I was a mean, hard, and tough Drill Instructor, and regrettably I did not always play by the rules. I admit that I did some things that were not in the rulebook, and unfortunately they came back to bite me.

> *I had not done what I was being charged with; however, my past indiscretions were coming back to haunt me. I was deserving of justice, but I needed mercy.*

While the prosecutor paraded recruit after recruit (fifty-three of them) on the witness stand, my freedom was slowly slipping away. Then it happened.

While being questioned, one of the recruits stopped in the middle of the inquiries and asked the prosecutor, "Are we testifying against Drill Instructor Sergeant Wilder?"

The prosecutor answered, "Yes, that is why we are having this trial!"

The recruit replied, "Drill Instructor Sergeant Wilder never told us to beat up the recruits, and he did not know we did it!"

The prosecutor immediately screamed, "Amnesty, amnesty for all the recruits!"

The judge cleared the courtroom, except for the prosecutor, the defense attorney, and me. He had each recruit—all fifty-three of them—come back in one at a time and tell what had happened. Of the fifty-three, thirty-seven stated after talking to the legal prosecuting team, they thought they should say the Drill Instructors wanted them to harm other recruits; however, none of the Drill Instructors actually told them to do that. They testified that I did not issue any order for them to harm the recruits; instead they did it on their own.

The judge reconvened the court and instructed the jury on what to strike and what charges were left. My defense lawyer and the military judge were amazing; the prosecutor's case was slipping away.

The trial ended, and the jury was released to deliberate. About three hours later, they returned with a verdict.

The foreman stood and intoned, "We the jury find Sergeant Gary Wilder not guilty of all charges but find him negligent that he should have known the recruits were being beaten. We fine him three hundred dollars and request he goes back to work (that is, training recruits)."

The judge agreed, and we did not appeal. I received justice, but mercy came in and said, "Step aside! I have this!"

I was and still am a believer in Christ, and although I was not living for Him at that time, He never left my side.

God has blessed me with a praying wife. No matter how low I fell during this process, she always lifted me up and prayed for me constantly. I watched as she cried throughout the three-day trial, but she never lost hope that I would be exonerated of the charges. I praised God for putting her in my life and continue to praise Him for her now.

Going through this ordeal was not the one-degree moment in my life. The experience allowed me to step back and regroup. Even though I was given the opportunity to return to training recruits, I refused it. The fire to train was gone, along with my motivation to even remain in the Marine Corps once my contract ended. Just as in land navigation, I had missed my objective. I had to shoot a back azimuth line with the compass for my life and regroup to see where I was going.

Shooting a Back Azimuth

A back azimuth is the opposite direction of an azimuth. Remember, an azimuth is focusing on an object and heading that direction. However, when you get lost, you must shoot a back azimuth so you can return to your known starting point. It is comparable to doing an about-face. "To obtain a back azimuth from an azimuth, you add 180 degrees if the azimuth is 180 degrees or less or subtract 180 degrees if the azimuth is 180 degrees or more. The back azimuth of 180 degrees may be stated as 0 degrees or 360 degrees."[25]

When doing a back azimuth, you must be very careful when adding and subtracting the 180 degrees. If there is a mathematical error, it could prove to be catastrophic with serious consequences.

It is the same when traveling through life. At times, I am so focused on my destination that I must take a step back and recalibrate to ensure I am going in the right direction. Steven Handel wrote, "To take a 'step back' simply means to give yourself time and be patient. Instead of reacting impulsively, wait for the dust to settle before making a choice or moving forward."[26]

This is what I had to do once the court-martial was concluded. I had to regroup, understand that I was still in Christ, and realize the old was gone and new things were coming in my life. I did not want to make a rash decision that could affect my future.

One-Degree Moment: Pull Up Your Bootstraps!

I still had just over two years remaining on my Marine Corps contract and about six months left on the Drill Instructor contract. As I waited for my Drill Instructor tour to end, I was assigned to the battalion headquarters. A change in leadership took place, and a new Sergeant Major took over. The new Sergeant Major was Lorin Rhaney, nicknamed "The Bear." He was a towering figure with a no-nonsense personality. He did not want to hear excuses. He just wanted to see results.

A couple months had passed, and I still had not met the Sergeant Major personally. I knew him only through group meetings and formations. One day while I was walking past his office with my head down, feeling dejected, he yelled, "Hey, Marine, what's your issue?"

I did not respond as I did not think he was talking to me.

He yelled again, "Hey, Sergeant, I'm talking to you! Get in my office now!"

As I entered his office, he asked, "What is your issue, and why are you walking around like you are defeated?"

"Sergeant Major I cannot believe I just went through all of this for nothing. They found me not guilty, and almost messed up my life!"

"Sergeant, I know I wasn't your Sergeant Major during the trial, but I followed this case, and you were fortunate to walk away intact!

You didn't lose your stripes or get any jail time; just a three-hundred dollar fine!"

"I hear you Sergeant Major, but it was wrong! They put me through all this and for what reason? I feel like my life is ruined! You don't get it Sergeant Major!"

As I continued to grumble, this is where my life changed.

Sergeant Major stood up, walked around his desk with that towering presence, and shouted, "Shut up!"

I guess my mind had left my body because I continued to talk.

He emphasized the phrase again, "Shut up!" But this time he used much more force. "Lock your body!" (stand at attention).

As I stood there, he punched me in the chest, knocking me back. He got in my face and said, "Sergeant, that's the last time I will hear any complaining from you! From this point, *pull up your bootstraps* and walk like the Marine that I know that you are and can become! You have a lot to offer to the Corps. From this point on, act like it! Now get out of my office and let this be the last time I see you walk like you are defeated!"

With a look of bewilderment, I responded, "Aye, Aye Sergeant Major!"

That moment changed my outlook on the Corps and propelled me to go on to have a successful career and success in life. John Maxwell wrote, "Vow to bounce back. No matter how many times you fall down, pick yourself up and keep going. Don't wait until you feel positive to move forward. Act your way into feeling good. That's the only way to start thinking more positively about yourself."[27]

Once I shook myself, lifted my head, and began to stride with purpose, I vowed not to let anyone or anything break my spirit to become successful with anything I wanted to accomplish. No one was going to write my story. I had read in Proverbs 24:16 (HCSB), "Though a righteous man falls seven times, he will get up." Although I fell, I was determined to get back up!

With this one-degree moment, I still chose not to return to the training platoons. Instead, I received orders to 1st Battalion, 5th Marines at Camp Pendleton California as a heavy machine gunner and Platoon Sergeant.

One-degree moments can come at the most inopportune times. They can lead to victory or defeat. In this case, through all I had experienced, this one-degree moment led me to victory. Incidentally, nearly eight years later Sergeant Major Rhaney and I crossed paths, and strangely enough, I was serving my second tour as a Drill Instructor, but this time training college students to become Marine Corps officers at Officer Candidates School in Quantico, Virginia.

I was now a Gunnery Sergeant (E-7) and serving as the Leadership Chief after completing two years with the training platoons in Charlie Company as a Sergeant Instructor and Platoon Sergeant. (Ironically, if you look back, it was on the Drill Field with Charlie Company where all this began!)

Noticing me, he said, "Gunny Wilder! Great to see you again."

"Likewise, Sergeant Major." We reflected on that moment in his office on the Drill Field.

"I see you didn't let the drill field court martial stop you from getting promoted. I am proud of you and the success you are having in the Corps!"

"Thanks Sergeant Major. You inspired me that day in your office telling me not to walk defeated but pull up my bootstraps while, at the same time, thumping me in my chest!"

We laughed and continued to conversate. Hearing those words from him cemented our relationship.

After his retirement, he and I became great friends, and to this day we continue to stay in touch with one another. He now serves as a minister at Shiloh Baptist Church (New Site) in Fredericksburg, Virginia.

God allowed me to retire from the Corps as a Master Sergeant (E-8) from the 3rd Light Armored Reconnaissance Battalion (Wolf Pack), Twenty-Nine Palms, California. From that one-degree moment, God called me into the gospel ministry. Additionally, I worked in the corporate world, and I am now the owner and president of an adult men's minor league football team (the Palm Beach Makos, Inc.) and vice president of Men2Boys Mentoring Program, Inc. I also worked for the government for a short stint. Currently I am publishing books and speaking around the country.

> *When we allow God to be the center of our dreams,*
> *He will propel us to victory.*

Let me be clear: God did not allow the court-martial to happen to humble me. I did this to myself because I allowed the enemy (the devil) to let pride take over and I was living an ungodly life. I was on an ego trip because of the power I had over recruits, and it led to my near demise. God showed me mercy through this situation.

The Praying Wife

While we were living in Fredericksburg, Virginia, when I was stationed at Quantico, Felecia brought the court-martial ordeal to a conclusion. We had gone on a date night to watch the newly released *Independence Day* movie. After the movie, we went to dinner and were discussing the part that Will Smith played as a Marine Corps pilot. I guess that triggered something in her, and we began to reflect on my career up to that point. She brought up the court-martial incident and how tough it was for her to watch me go through it.

She said, "As I prayed for you, I knew God would get us through it, but I prayed that He would show you something through it. Even though it was hard to endure, that court-martial was the best thing that happened to you."

Her comments caught me by surprise. I wasn't expecting to hear that, and I asked her to explain.

She continued, "You were letting the power as a Drill Instructor make you into someone you were not, and I saw that you were not the same. During the court-martial, you returned to being you, and the ordeal allowed you to see your true self. It was hard to watch, but through it, God is now using you to share His gospel."

Even though I was taken aback by her comments, she was right on point. Proverbs 18:22 (CSB) says, "A man who finds a wife, finds a good thing, and obtains favor from the Lord."

God gave me a great wife who is truthful to speak into my life. Having someone speak truth into your life is important for obtaining lasting success. I had to change me, and that court-martial allowed me to look in the mirror of life. As we look at ourselves, one of the most difficult things to do is change ourselves.

> *If I wanted to see a change with my situation, I had to change me.*

If you find yourself going through an ordeal, ask, "God, what are you trying to show me through this situation?" God may show you or lead someone else to show you, just as He did with my wife, what He wants you to learn through the ordeal. Whatever He shows you, act on it and allow Him to catapult you to the success. "And we know that for those who love God all things work together for good, for those who are called according to his purpose" (Romans 8:28 ESV).

For me, the power of a praying wife made a difference, a wife who loves God and allows Him to use her for His purpose. Prayer changes things!

Direction 6
Final Direction

Old Buck

I am from North Carolina, which has many rural dirt roads. When I think of North Carolina, I am reminded of an anonymous story of a man driving down a dirt road near a farm. It was raining, and the road was slippery. The man's car slid off the road and into a ditch. He tried for a while to get it out, but to no avail. Across a field, he saw a house with a light on, and in the rain, he jogged over to the house and knocked on the door.

An old farmer wearing bib overalls came out and asked, "What's the trouble?"

"I ran off the road and my car is stuck in the ditch. Any assistance that you could give me would be appreciated!"

The farmer said, "Well, I have an ol' mule in the barn named Buck, and we can see if he can help."

The man replied, "Any assistance would be great!"

So the farmer took old Buck and hooked him to the car. Then he walked to the right side of Buck and said, "Now, Tom, pull! Now, Harry, pull! Now, John, pull! Now, Buck, pull!"

Ol' Buck reared down and pulled the car out of the ditch.

The man was grateful but a little confused. He said to the famer, "I thought you said your mule's name was Buck. Why did you call out those other names?"

The farmer hooked his thumbs into his overall straps and explained, "Well, you see, ol' Buck is blind, and if he knew he had to pull this car by himself, you would still be stuck!"

Teamwork

When I get just one-degree off the path to my destination, I may need assistance getting back on track. Just as ol' Buck thought he had a team to help him pull, I need someone to help pull me out of my situation and direct me back to the path I need to travel. In the last direction, Sergeant Major Rhaney helped me realize I was off course. He gave me the nudge I needed to set my compass on the right azimuth.

We are not in this world alone, and we need the aid of others to give us the correct grid coordinates. Helen Keller stated, "Alone we can do little; Together we can do much"[28] Ol' Buck knew that without teamwork, he could not accomplish the task that was ahead of him, and it is the same with us. Without the team, we cannot accomplish the task.

No one is a self-made person or millionaire because it took someone to make the person they are, and it took someone else's money to make that individual a millionaire!

In the Marine Corps, like the other branches of the military, our number-one focus is the team. Everything we say, do, or write speaks about the team. The Corps has fourteen leadership traits and eleven principles that every Marine must know and carry in our hearts. However, these traits and principles are nothing without the team. Any Marine placed as a leader not only leads themselves but receives input from the team they are leading.

When I say that we lead ourselves, the first leadership principle is "know yourself and seek self-improvement."[29] Understanding who I am as a leader will help me understand the Marines I am leading.

Knowing this aids in training them as a team, which is principle number seven, "Train your Marines as a team."[30]

> *Teamwork is the essence of who we are as Marines, and every leader gets their team involved, which leads the team to being committed to the mission in front of them.*

Every Marine, once they have crossed the sands of boot camp or officer training, is on a quest to discover who they are as a person and a quest to create a solid team. President Ronald Reagan stated in a speech he gave in 1985, "Some people spend an entire lifetime wondering if they made a difference in the world. But the Marines don't have that problem."[31]

Seeking self-improvement is a conscious decision for every Marine. Once self-improvement is underway, then we seek to transfer that discovery to building a team. We are not looking for individual superstars but a well-oiled machine that will accomplish any task, in any climate, at any destination around the world.

The Art of Discovery

Ecclesiastes 4:9 (CEV) shows us that "you are better off to have a friend than to be all alone, because then you will get more enjoyment out of what you earn."

It takes teamwork to help us with our direction. John Maxwell commented, "Teamwork makes the dream work."[32] As we take this journey, whether we start out alone or venture with a team, we will begin to discover new things about ourselves and what we have within us. Our lives are full of discoverable moments.

As children, we set out to discover the world around us through adventure and social interactions. In a study from the Encyclopedia on Early Childhood Development entitled, "The Development of

Theory of Mind in Early Childhood," Astington and Edward write, "Children's awareness of thoughts, wants and feelings is inferred from what they say and do in naturalistic and experimental situations. Natural settings show the child's abilities to interact with others in the real world."[33] Discovery and interaction are how we begin to uncover our gifts and talents.

As you have traveled through this book, my prayer is that you have read something that has stirred you to see your one-degree moment. If not, my prayer is that something written will jump-start you toward your purpose and destiny. God has a desire to bless your future and to give you hope. Jeremiah 29:11 (CEV) states it nicely, "I will bless you with a future filled with hope—a future of success, not of suffering."

To give your future a start, you must look at where you are and then write down where you see yourself going. John Maxwell said, "Examine your expectations for that area. Write them down. Are they realistic? Do you expect to do everything perfectly? Do you expect to succeed on the first try? How many mistakes should you expect to make before you succeed? Adjust your expectations."[34]

Writing our vision will allow others to see it and then assist us with it. Look again at Habakkuk 2 2:2–3 (CEV), "Then the Lord told me: 'I will give you my message in the form of a vision. Write it clearly enough to be read at a glance. At the time I have decided, my words will come true. You can trust what I say about the future. It may take a long time but keep on waiting— it will happen!'"

What we desire may not come about right away. We have to wait for it and believe the seed we have sowed will bring a harvest. When we plant a seed, it does not immediately give fruit. We have to allow the pressure of the dirt, water for nourishment, and sunrays to allow it to grow to produce the fruit.

It's the same with our dreams, visions, and gifts. We have to allow God to apply the pressure, Christ to give the sun, and the Holy Spirit to provide the nourishment for it to bring forth the fruit. If we dig up the seed before it has time to germinate, then the fruit we are expecting will not develop. With anything planted, the storms of life will come against it to prevent it from producing any fruit.

Remember, sometimes life comes at us quickly and hard, which could stunt our fruit's growth. When life throws punches at us, we have to be resilient and throw punches back. Like I said, life doesn't always pass us by. Sometimes it runs us over!

> *When this happens, what is important is how we respond. We have to get up when we've been mown down!*

This is where refocusing on your purpose and destiny comes into play. Although you may be one degree off target, shoot a back azimuth (take a step back), recalibrate (re-evaluate), and do not allow situations and circumstances to dictate your direction. God has a plan for you. It is up to you to follow the plan and to act on it. James Sawyer cited the purpose of man,

> There exists a deep-seated desire, a compulsive drive, because man is made in the image of God to appreciate the beauty of the world (on an aesthetic level); to know the character, composition and meaning of the world (on an academic and philosophical level); and to discern its purpose and destiny (on a theological level) ... Man has an inborn inquisitiveness and capacity to learn how everything in his experience can be integrated to make a whole.[35]

We have the propensity to want to learn and discover new things. It is the same with our purpose and destiny. Once we discover it, it is time to act on it. You might say, "I haven't discovered my purpose." That is okay. Just begin doing something! Your purpose will rise to the top of your conscious thinking. Start by volunteering or getting involved in something positive that aligned with your dreams and visions. If you need to get a job because of finances, then get a job, but work it with the objective of leaving it to go to work on your dream and purpose. God has placed your purpose in a place where you cannot miss it.

The Hidden Future

When I think about my future, I often reflect on my past. How I reflect on the past will determine what I think of my future. I can look at my past in a positive or negative light. If positive, I tend to see a positive future. If negative, I could paint a negative future. I have to choose to look at a negative past and create a positive future. Someone who looks at a negative past and sees a grim future still has the choice to determine how the future unfolds.

Do not allow anyone to write your story but you!

Although the past might have been bleak, see it as a learning experience rather than a failure. Job 8:7 (CEV) gives insight by showing that "your future will be brighter by far than your past." This verse is not saying that your past did not exist, but that your past will not dictate your future.

Former South African President Nelson Mandela stated, "I could not imagine that the future I was walking toward could compare in any way to the past that I was leaving behind."[36] As a political prisoner for twenty-seven years, President Mandela could have given up on his future, but instead he saw the positive in his future.

President Mandela knew the gift that was inside of him. He never lost sight of whom he was nor what he could become even while imprisoned and working arduous tasks. He made a habit of encouraging himself in the midst of his trials. Ask yourself these questions:

- What kind of habits do I have?
- When faced with challenging situations, do I have a habit of complaining, getting discouraged, or pointing the finger at others as to why things did not turn out as I had planned?
- Am I seeing the positive side of how my future can turn out?

That is what President Mandela did. He was in control of the habits that formed his life, and we are in control of the habits that shape our lives.

I was listening to a message from Dr. Myles Munroe entitled "Manifest Your Gift." During the message, he talked about habits and gifts. As I reflected on President Mandela and the message from Dr. Munroe, the two aligned themselves. Dr. Munroe declared, "We don't decide our future, we decide our habits, and our habits decide our future."[37]

That is a true statement. The habits we choose will determine the future that we will possess. For example, if we have a habit of coming home from our jobs, sitting back in the chair, and watching television for the rest of the evening, what future are we creating? If we have a habit of hanging out with friends at a local bar or club, what are we achieving?

On the other hand, if we are in the habit of leaving our jobs and working on gifts or getting involved with things that are productive for success, that habit will change our destiny. Remember, we are seeking to keep our compass pointed in the right direction to prevent getting one-degree off our purpose.

Dr. Munroe continued his message by saying, "Each of you came to this earth because there's something that earth needed that God hid inside of you ... God hid your future (gift) in a place He knew you wouldn't miss it. He placed it inside of you!"[38]

When I think of my past or future, what internal thing connects them both? The internal force is my gift. Every single human has a gift within them. Each of us has a gift; however, it is up to us to manifest or use that gift. Romans 12:6 (CEV) describes it this way, "God has also given each of us different gifts to use." What is the gift I am carrying that this generation needs?

When I go to an event, whether sports, movies, stage plays, and so forth, I am not paying to see a player or actor. I am paying to see their gifts. If I am watching a sporting event, I am giving my money to see that athlete run, swim, shoot the basketball, or win a championship. I do not know them personally, but I know the gifts they possess at that moment.

Watching them use their gifts can also be a source of encouragement for me. Something they do may inspire me to go after my own dream or desire.

Ask this question, "What is the one thing that brings joy and excitement to my life?" Pastor Joel Osteen stated, "Your gift may seem insignificant, but when you release it, God will multiply it. He will multiply your talent, your influence, your resources."[39]

What is your gift? 2 Timothy 1:6 (NKJV) says, "Therefore, I remind you to stir up the gift of God which is in you." The gift will demand commitment to see it through to completion.

Let's examine the word *commitment*. Commitment means to be dedicated to a cause or an activity, to be devoted or faithful to it. One of our Marine Corps advertisements says, "We don't accept applications. Only commitment."[40] Commitment is also one of the core values of the Marine Corps.

Many people are not committed. If something does not work right away, rather than being creative to try something new, many just give up without seeing it through. Unfortunately, by not seeing it through, many people cut their gifts short. Imagine, if Bill Gates had not followed his dream, the world might not be using Microsoft. However, he stayed committed to his dream and gift.

Bishop T. D. Jakes said in his message titled "Committed," "I would hate to live and die and never know what would happen if I ever committed myself to anything."[41] We have to remain committed to the gift within us. We owe it to the world and our generation!

This is what President Mandela did by staying focused on his dream and the gift of leadership that was inside of him. This is what we must do as well. Stay focused and committed to the gift that God has placed inside of us. The gift is not for our benefit, but for others to grow as a result of it.

Bishop Rick Thomas stated, "God has people waiting on you to get your act together so they can become what God has created them to be."[42] We are the catalyst for someone to manifest their gift. Therefore, we have to act now so they can become what God has designed them to become.

You may be saying, "I am at a place where I am not able to use my gift." God said in Proverbs 18:16 (NKJV), "A man's gift makes room for him, and brings him before great men." When we stay focused on our gifts, God will multiply them and ensure they will fit where He wants them to fit. You have to be doing something to discover the gift within you. As we begin doing something, God will provide opportunities that will reveal our gifts, which will allow us to share it with our generation.

For years, even while serving in the Marine Corps, I did not know what gift I had within me, and it was frustrating. But I kept trying different things until one day I started doing something that brought me joy, peace, and fulfillment. I realized that I have the gift of encouragement. Being able to assist others to find their fulfillment gives me fulfillment. My gift affords me opportunities to speak to audiences and share a word of encouragement. The question I am often asked is, "Are you getting paid for doing it?" Sometimes I do, and other times I do not. If I am looking to get paid for my gift, then it is probably not my gift.

> *Remember, your gift will make room for you. Your gift should bring value to others. When it brings value, it will make you valuable, and when you are valuable, people will pay for your value.*

That is what happened with President Mandela. He was not seeking payment; nor was he seeking fame. He was seeking justice for an unjust society in South Africa with apartheid rule. As a result of staying focused on his gift, he became valuable, which led him to be the giant of a man he was destined to become.

Do not allow the system of the world to steal your gift; they could be buried with you. We must keep our hopes, dreams, ideas, concepts, and strategies alive so future generations can benefit from them! Our generation needs the gifts and dreams that are inside of you!

There is greatness within you! Do not allow the weight of the world to smother the gifts and dreams inside of you. This is your time; this is your moment! Shake the dust off your dreams, pull up your bootstraps, and allow God to manifest the gift within you. Start now!

Invictus

We are depending on you to share your gifts with us so we can fulfill what we are destined to. Think about what would have happened if Michael Jordon had given up basketball after not making his high school basketball team. We would have never witnessed his gift of basketball. If President Mandela had given up, we would not have witnessed a nation drawn together.

You may feel like you are more than one-degree off track, but don't be discouraged. You can get back on course to accomplish what God has placed within you. I don't know whether you are reading this book at a restaurant, coffee shop, park, or jail or if it's 2:00 a.m. and you are lying in bed. Regardless of where you are, if you are not where you want to be at this point in your life, allow this book to be the one-degree catalyst to jump-start you on the road to your purpose and destiny. You must find what encourages you.

President Mandela recited a poem that kept him encouraged. Other than the Bible, which is my complete source of strength, this poem is one I have recited for more than thirty years. When I was literally facing my trial or I want to encourage others, I recited it. It is a poem by British poet William Ernest Henley entitled "Invictus." It reads,

> Out of the night that covers me,
> Black as the pit from pole to pole,
> I thank whatever gods may be
> For my unconquerable soul.
>
> In the fell clutch of circumstance
> I have not winced nor cried aloud.
> Under the bludgeoning's of chance
> My head is bloody, but unbowed.
>
> Beyond this place of wrath and tears
> Looms but the Horror of the shade,
> And yet the menace of the years
> Finds and shall find me unafraid.
>
> It matters not how strait the gate,

How charged with punishments the scroll,
I am the master of my fate,
I am the captain of my soul.

In closing, my challenge to you is to be the master of your fate and the captain of your soul. We all have or may be having our one-degree moment. Just know that you are in control of your future and destiny.

When I was faced with my situation as a Drill Instructor, I could have bowed my head and quit. Instead I learned through Sergeant Major Rhaney that I was in charge of my fate and destiny and that I needed to write my own story. Staying focused on God and having the right mentors in my life allowed me to right my ship and take control of my destiny!

It is the same for you, wherever you may find yourself. You are the captain of your own destiny! Do not allow anyone or anything to stop you from completing it.

> *You may lose your job, but your gift is still in you. You may lose your home, but your gift is still in you. You may lose a relationship, but your gift is still within you!*

Remember, your gifts will make room for you and bring you before great people! Keep people around you (mentors) who encourage you and help you discover the gift already inside you. "The most important thing in life is not knowing everything, it's having the phone number of somebody who does!"[43]

You may be one-degree off, but you are the master of your fate and the captain of your soul! Take ownership of your life's direction. Shoot a back azimuth and get back on course!

Today, you will hit your objective, which will lead you to your purpose and destiny and bring complete victory in all that you seek or desire! Today I want you to shoot your back azimuth so you can step into a directional moment to get realigned, readjusted, and repositioned so you can get one-degree back on track! *Blessings on your journey as you unleash your focus!*

Endnotes

Direction One

1   OrenHarari, *The Leadership Secrets of Colin Powell* (McGraw-Hill Education), 12.
2   United States Marine Corps, "Mission of the Marine Corps," accessed March 12, 2019, https://www.Marines.com/who-we-are/our-purpose.html.
3   Dave Logan, *Tribal Leadership Revised Edition* (Harper Business), 71.
4   Bill Hull, *The Complete Book of Discipleship: On Being and Making Followers of Christ* (The Navigators Reference Library 1, 2014).
5   Martin Sanders, *The Power of Mentoring: Shaping People Who Will Shape the World* (Camp Hill, Penn.: WingSpread Publishers, 2009), 2.
6   Homer, and Samuel Butler, "The Internet Classics Archive: The Odyssey by Homer," http://classics.mit.edu/Homer/odyssey.html.
7   Martin Sanders, 157.
8   Matthew Floding, "What Is Theological Field Education?" in *Welcome to Theological Field Education!*, ed. Matthew Floding (Lanham, Md.: Rowman & Littlefield, 2014), 11.

Direction Two

9   Pastor Joel Osteen on "Dreams"
10 Martin Sanders, 186.
11 Carl Bain, Jerome Beaty, and J. Paul Hunter, "A Raisin in the Sun (Langston Hughes)," in *The Norton Introduction to Literature* (New York: W. W. Norton, 1981), 600.
12 Jack O. Balswick and Judith K. Balswick, *Family: A Christian Perspective on the Contemporary Home* (Grand Rapids, Mich.: Baker Academic), 2014.
13 Marine Corps Traits and Principles.
14 Najja Parker, "Do You Daydream? That May Mean You're Sharper and More Creative than Your Peers, Study Says," https://www.ajc.com/news/world/you-daydream-that-may-mean-you-sharper-and-more-creative-than-your-peers-study-says/awHQEglmkeOV93CzB1vl9I/.

15 "Henry Louis Mencken Funny Quotes," https://www.coolfunnyquotes. com/author/henry-louis-mencken/come-with-nothing.

Direction Three

16 Sports & Fitness Industry Association, "SGMA Says The Olympics Do Impact Sports Participation," accessed May 11, 2019, https:// www.sfia.org/press/431_SGMA-Says-The-Olympics-Do-Impact-Sports-Participation.
17 Steve Mueller, "Bruce Lee – Focus," http://www.planetofsuccess. com/blog/2016/inspiring-focus-quotes/.
18 United States Marine Corps, "United States Marines Corps Commitment," https://www.Marines.com.
19 Rick Thomas, "Sermon – Why Do I Exist," http://www.abundantlife. tv/media.
20 "A Quote by Abraham Lincoln," https://www.goodreads.com/ quotes/5851097-and-in-the-end-it-s-not-the-years-in-your.

Direction Four

21 Dale Carnegie, "A Quote by Dale Carnegie," https://www.goodreads. com/quotes/31235-remember-today-is-the-tomorrow-you-worried-about-yesterday.
22 Neil T. Anderson, *Discipleship Counseling*, ed. Benjamin Unseth (Ventura, Calif.: Regal, 2003), 53.
23 "Jimmy Dean Quotes," https://www.brainyquote.com/authors/ jimmy-dean-quotes.

Direction Five

24 Woodrow Kroll, "Justice," https://www.tumblr.com/search/woodrow kroll.
25 United States Marine Corps, "Land Navigation. Back Azimuth," Officer Candidates School. Quantico, Va., 2011.
26 Steven Handel, "The Art of Taking a Step Back," https://www. theemotionmachine.com/the-art-of-taking-a-step-back.
27 John C. Maxwell, *Failing Forward: How To Make The Most Of Your Mistakes* (Thomas Nelson Publishers, 2000), 33–34.

Direction Six

28 John Leo Weber, "Teamwork Quotes: 25 Best Inspirational Quotes About Working Together (*Helen Keller*)," https://www.projectmanager.com/blog/teamwork-quotes-25-best-inspirational-quotes-working-together.

29 "Research Guides: QPME: History and Traditions of the United States Marine Corps: Ethics, Values, and Leadership Development: 4. Qualities," https://grc-usmcu.libguides.com/pme/qpme/Marine-corps-ethics-values-leadership-development/qualities.

30 History and Traditions of the United States Marine Corps.

31 Ronald Reagan, "U.S. Department of Defense," https://archive.defense.gov/speeches/speech.aspx?speechid=1815#:

32 John C. Maxwell, *Teamwork Makes the Dream Work* (Nashville, Tenn.: J. Countryman, 2002).

33 J. W. Astington and M. J. Edward, "The Development of Theory of Mind in Early Childhood," http://www.child-encyclopedia.com/social-cognition/according-experts/development-theory-mind-early-childhood.

34 John C. Maxwell, *Failing Forward: How To Make The Most Of Your Mistakes* (Thomas Nelson Publishers, 2000), 33–34.

35 M. James Sawyer, *The Survivor's Guide to Theology* (Grand Rapids, Mich.: Zondervan, 2006), 133.

36 Nelson Mandela, *Long Walk to Freedom: The Autobiography of Nelson Mandela* (London: Little, Brown and Company, 2014).

37 Melissa Ozuna, "Manifest Your Gift," Dr. Myles Munroe, https://www.youtube.com/watch?v=vVUFqBcJ68s.

38 Ibid.

39 Joel Osteen, https://twitter.com/JoelOsteen/status/1038774589319467009.

40 Defense Department, "Defense Science Board and Senate Armed Services Committee Meetings (Marine Corps Advertisement)," *PsycEXTRA Dataset*, 2007, https://doi.org/10.1037/e619202007-003.

41 The Potters House, "Committed," https://www.youtube.com/watch?v=zA-i-bv10OU

42 Thomas, "Sermon – Why Do I Exist."

43 Anonymous.